NO TIME TO LOSE

A SEARCH FOR WORK/LIFE BALANCE
CURATED BY MILENA PLACENTILE

NO TIME TO LOSE
A search for work/life balance

13 JUNE - 26 JULY 2008
Curated by Milena Placentile

Peacock Visual Arts
21 Castle Street
Aberdeen AB11 5BQ
peacockvisualarts.com

Charity SC 56235

Published by Peacock Visual Arts,
Aberdeen, Scotland

Editors
Milena Placentile, Monika Vykoukal

Essays
Jim Colquhoun, Toru Yamamori

Photographs
The Artists, Thomas Kettle

Design
Jess Koroscil

ISBN 978-0-9555524-6-5

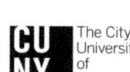
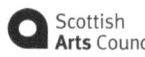

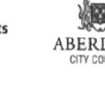
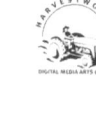

NDERSTAND. I'VE BEEN PRETTY SPAZZED OUT WITH MY
ELSE ON MY WORKLOAD AGENDA. OR AT LEAST, I CAN
, SO I WANT TO TRY TO NAG THE BOSS IF I CAN... THIS
21. JUST SO I CAN PLAN MY TIME, CAN YOU PLEASE LET
IFFERENCES IN TIME ZONES, I JUST RECEIVED IT NOW,
SHORTLY, AND IT IS GOING TO BE A FAIRLY LONG DAY.
A BIT OF A BREAK IN SOME WAY. SO FINALLY GOT TO
T TO MY WORK ON WEDNESDAY! THANKS. X JUST LEFT
OW ASKED TO WORK ON TECHNICAL DETAILS HE ASKED
Y OF THOSE TECHNICAL THINGS MYSELF... THANKS SO
IN A BIT OF A BAD MOOD, BUT HOPEFULLY SNAP OUT
ONCEPT LATELY. I WISH YOU ALL THE BEST!! I WON'T
SELF OUT OF THE POT AND INTO THE FIRE. LET'S HOPE
THE STUFF FOR WHICH THERE IS NO ACTUAL PROCESS!
ALING TIME IS MYSELF... I JUST REMEMBERED ALL THE
D IS REELING... I SHOULD GET BACK TO MY JOB-RELAT-
TO CRACK UNDER THE PRESSURE OF TOO MUCH TO DO
LL OF THEM TODAY! I'M GOING TO STOP TYPING NOW.
DIATELY. I FEEL TORN IN TOO MANY DIRECTIONS, AND
THE FACT THAT IT'S THE ONLY THING ACTUALLY SUP-
MUCH GOING ON AND MY BRAIN IS GETTING SQUISHY.
N I GET BACK, THAT'S GOING TO BE SUCKING WHAT'S
RE TODAY BEFORE I LEAVE...I'VE BEEN KNOWN TO SAVE
E THINGS OUT SOONER, BUT I'VE BEEN OVERWHELMED
NDERSTAND. I'VE BEEN PRETTY SPAZZED OUT WITH MY
G ELSE ON MY WORKLOAD AGENDA. OR AT LEAST, I CAN
, SO I WANT TO TRY TO NAG THE BOSS IF I CAN... THIS
21. JUST SO I CAN PLAN MY TIME, CAN YOU PLEASE LET
DIFFERENCES IN TIME ZONES, I JUST RECEIVED IT NOW,
SHORTLY, AND IT IS GOING TO BE A FAIRLY LONG DAY.
A BIT OF A BREAK IN SOME WAY. SO FINALLY GOT TO
T TO MY WORK ON WEDNESDAY! THANKS. X JUST LEFT
OW ASKED TO WORK ON TECHNICAL DETAILS HE ASKED
Y OF THOSE TECHNICAL THINGS MYSELF... THANKS SO
IN A BIT OF A BAD MOOD, BUT HOPEFULLY SNAP OUT
ONCEPT LATELY. I WISH YOU ALL THE BEST!! I WON'T
SELF OUT OF THE POT AND INTO THE FIRE. LET'S HOPE
THE STUFF FOR WHICH THERE IS NO ACTUAL PROCESS!
ALING TIME IS MYSELF... I JUST REMEMBERED ALL THE
D IS REELING... I SHOULD GET BACK TO MY JOB-RELAT-
TO CRACK UNDER THE PRESSURE OF TOO MUCH TO DO
LL OF THEM TODAY! I'M GOING TO STOP TYPING NOW.
DIATELY. I FEEL TORN IN TOO MANY DIRECTIONS, AND
THE FACT THAT IT'S THE ONLY THING ACTUALLY SUP-
MUCH GOING ON AND MY BRAIN IS GETTING SQUISHY.
N I GET BACK, THAT'S GOING TO BE SUCKING WHAT'S
RE TODAY BEFORE I LEAVE...I'VE BEEN KNOWN TO SAVE
SE THINGS OUT SOONER, BUT I'VE BEEN OVERWHELMED
NDERSTAND. I'VE BEEN PRETTY SPAZZED OUT WITH MY
G ELSE ON MY WORKLOAD AGENDA. OR AT LEAST, I CAN
, SO I WANT TO TRY TO NAG THE BOSS IF I CAN... THIS
21. JUST SO I CAN PLAN MY TIME, CAN YOU PLEASE LET
DIFFERENCES IN TIME ZONES, I JUST RECEIVED IT NOW,
SHORTLY, AND IT IS GOING TO BE A FAIRLY LONG DAY.
A BIT OF A BREAK IN SOME WAY. SO FINALLY GOT TO
T TO MY WORK ON WEDNESDAY! THANKS. X JUST LEFT
OW ASKED TO WORK ON TECHNICAL DETAILS HE ASKED
Y OF THOSE TECHNICAL THINGS MYSELF... THANKS SO
D IN A BIT OF A BAD MOOD, BUT HOPEFULLY SNAP OUT
CONCEPT LATELY. I WISH YOU ALL THE BEST!! I WON'T
SELF OUT OF THE POT AND INTO THE FIRE. LET'S HOPE
THE STUFF FOR WHICH THERE IS NO ACTUAL PROCESS!
EALING TIME IS MYSELF... I JUST REMEMBERED ALL THE
D IS REELING... I SHOULD GET BACK TO MY JOB-RELAT-
TO CRACK UNDER THE PRESSURE OF TOO MUCH TO DO
LL OF THEM TODAY! I'M GOING TO STOP TYPING NOW.
DIATELY. I FEEL TORN IN TOO MANY DIRECTIONS, AND
THE FACT THAT IT'S THE ONLY THING ACTUALLY SUP-
MUCH GOING ON AND MY BRAIN IS GETTING SQUISHY.
N I GET BACK, THAT'S GOING TO BE SUCKING WHAT'S
RE TODAY BEFORE I LEAVE...I'VE BEEN KNOWN TO SAVE
SE THINGS OUT SOONER, BUT I'VE BEEN OVERWHELMED
NDERSTAND. I'VE BEEN PRETTY SPAZZED OUT WITH MY
G ELSE ON MY WORKLOAD AGENDA. OR AT LEAST, I CAN
, SO I WANT TO TRY TO NAG THE BOSS IF I CAN... THIS
21. JUST SO I CAN PLAN MY TIME, CAN YOU PLEASE LET
DIFFERENCES IN TIME ZONES, I JUST RECEIVED IT NOW,
SHORTLY, AND IT IS GOING TO BE A FAIRLY LONG DAY.

CONTENTS

INTRODUCTION

MONIKA VYKOUKAL

At least since the industrialisation of the 1800s, workers' struggle has centered on limits to labour time, as epitomised in the struggle for the eight-hour day, which was won in most European and North American countries, as well as Australia and New Zealand, in the course of the last 150 years[1]. However, while the historic images of factory workers appear strikingly different from the experience of today's office and retail jobs, and despite the hard-won legal frameworks, overwork and its negative consequences for workers persist. Indeed, workers not only generate additional profit through unpaid overtime, but also insist in surveys that their extra hours are self-imposed, and that only their ambition or inefficiency are the cause of what is obviously a personal choice (CIPD, 2009, para. 10). This in the face of revelations, such as the ones in the documentary film *Wal-Mart: The High Cost of Low Prices* (Robert Greenwald, USA, 2005) that the understaffing of the shop floors of one of the largest global corporations is a systemic strategy of management to maximise profit. With figures suggesting that the number of workers putting in unpaid hours constitutes a substantial part of the workforce[2], and the increase in workload for those who remain in employment and have to make up for those laid off during the current recession (Baker, 2009; Woods, 2009), it seems clear that this is not merely the free choice of just so many atomised individuals.

In her essay, Canadian curator Milena Placentile introduces her thinking behind the development of *No Time to Lose* outlining such global developments, the causes of which have been summed up in a recent study (Burke, R. J. & Cooper, C. L., 2008) on overwork as "the pressure on companies to decrease their labour force and increase workloads", together with "the rise in consumerism and the decline of trade union power" (Kinman, 2009, para. 7). In the meantime, the ideology of free-market neoliberalism underpinning those developments remains on course, with a primer for advocates on the website of UK-based think-tank The Adam Smith Institute earlier this year proclaiming, for example, that "it is also important that we continue to make the case that it was not unbridled free markets, but rather interventionist governments which caused the 2008 crisis" (Clougherty, 2009, para. 7). Yet, as geographer and social theorist David Harvey points out, the success of ideologies such as neoliberalism also depends on their appeal to those which they in fact

1. The UK remains a notable exception as it retains an 'opt-out' clause from the European Community's Working Time Regulations, allowing companies "to ask employees to agree to work more than 48 hours a week" (The Chartered Institute for Personnel and Development, 2009).

2. A recent report on the British Trades Union Council's *Worksmart* website indicates: "The TUC has calculated that 5. 24 million people across the UK worked unpaid overtime in 2008, bringing its total value across the UK to a record £26. 9 billion - the highest number since records began in 1992" (Trades Union Council, 2009, para. 1).

disadvantage, but upon whose support they depend (Hofmeyr, 2005, p. 22). For neoliberalism, this appeal centers on the purported connection between the unregulated market and values of individual freedom and human dignity.

In line with those tenets, many of us now toil under a new paradigm of work, distinguished by our freedom from traditional drudgery, and a seemingly autonomous choice of creative permanent productivity, aided by new technologies. Contestations of this encroachment of work in all aspects of our lives, such as those raised by Japanese social policy researcher, Toru Yamamori, and by Scottish artist, Jim Colquhoun, in their contributions, range from the notion of a basic income, to the radical claim of striving for a life of creatively meaningful play in opposition to the inherently oppressive character of labouring. At present, this desire for pleasurable activity is increasingly contained and redirected to form one's professional calling. This surface of free choice and fulfillment quickly disappears when confronted with the (not so very) hidden forces propelling the new work culture in a ruthlessly competitive context where both full-time and long-term employment are long on the wane.

These notions of work also come with claims to a way of self-actualization through 'creativity'. 'Creativity' is, as shown by James Heartfield quoting the philosopher, economist, and psychoanalyst Cornelius Castoriadis,

in fact even a necessary component of mass production in factories, which already "rely(ies) upon the conscious and willing participation of the worker, on his capacity to understand and do much more than he is supposed to" (2008, p. 32). However, as opposed to the "defence of skills and the struggle against alienation" of previous generations, argues Heartfield, "our yearning for creativity is how we experience the problem of alienation in a highly individualised society." He concludes that, with regards to creativity in work, "as long as it is organised as private enterprise, then it will continue to be creativity at the behest of someone else, which quickly turns to routine drudgery" (p. 32).

Following from such considerations, *No Time to Lose* includes an analysis of the work of the artist as well as that of the arts professional, not as a 'special' position, but as 'yet another' job. The job of the artist and the conflict of creative play and labour are also more specifically the focus of Jim Colquhoun's intervention. As outlined by Diedrich Diederichsen (2008)[3]:

3. Diederichsen's text, in its entirety, constitutes a pertinent reflection on art and work in capitalism, but it is beyond the scope of this introduction to bring his analysis to bear upon the details of this project.

the curricula vitae of artists increasingly resemble those of other highly qualified specialized workers. [. . .] In the United States and other neoliberal areas of the world, financing this general component of labor that is socially necessary for the production of art has become the responsibility of the artists themselves, who take out loans to pay their way through school and, as it were, invest the income they will only receive later into their prior education. In this sense, artists are entrepreneurs who pursue their own material interest and later that of others. The alternate model (traditionally followed in Europe) effectively casts artists as civil servants or government employees and hence, at least indirectly, bound to a conception of the common good (p. 34).

With this perspective, *No Time to Lose* aims to connect our individual experiences in a meaningful way with those of others. Here a particular challenge, which also emerges in Placentile's essay, is how to connect the particular details of our working conditions with collective and systemic levels. In short, how to move both our understandings, and potentially our actions beyond the perspective of the good work ethic, which hides its exploitative underpinnings in a rhetoric of self-fulfillment or social usefulness.

In her analysis of the difficulties in developing any 'precarity-based'[4] activism, writer and researcher, Marina Vishmidt, describes this double-bind:

> The more intimate the encroachment of de-regulated and all-pervasive work on life, the stricter the psychic barriers between them, in line with a state of affairs that doesn't seem to provide much of an opening for collective social action and promotes de facto individual solutions. Hence: the unorganisability of 'chainworkers', who would decline to identify with their jobs to the minimal extent needed to organise for better working conditions, and freelancers, who, in common with most of the indentured and illusorily free working population, are skeptical about taking time out of procuring and completing short-term contracts to partake of a political engagement they may perceive as vain." (2007, pp. 290-291).

4. For a discussion on the notion of precarity see, for example, the interview with Alex Foti by Andreas Gustavsson titled Time for a new political slogan in *Taking the Matter into Common Hands* by Billing J., Lind, M. & Nilsson, L. (Eds.) (2007). London: Black Dog Publishing. pp. 41-47.

5. Be they next door or online.

6. This is a not entirely intentional, somewhat oblique quote of the manifesto Black, B. (1985). *The Abolition of Work*. Port Townsend: Loompanics Unlimited. Retrieved 12 September 2009 from http://www. spunk.org/library/writers/black/sp000156. txt.

This book, and the exhibition it documents, thus constitutes a specific exploration based on our experiences and sectors, and the contexts of the UK, Canada, and the United States respectively. In the installations and performances, some of which took the project into spaces beyond the gallery, Amy Alexander, Cathy Busby, Anja Hertenberger & Anja Steidinger, Saki Satom, Abigail Schoneboom, and Tobaron Waxman document and invite others to share specific work situations, as well as to play with, in, and perhaps even against them. Yet, just like all contributors to this project, they and their work nonetheless remain, for now, caught in the contemporary conditions of art and labour, where art functions "as an ideal object for reinvestment, be it through cultural-political instrumentalisation or through financial speculation [while still] capable of articulating content and enabling aesthetic experience independently of their commodity form" (Diederichsen, p. 25, 44). Thus, *No Time to Lose* does not claim to represent the hard edge of exploitation elsewhere, or to somehow have found an escape, or way for a radical break beyond the current working conditions, but would like to be a reminder to ourselves and our friends and neighbours[5] that it might be time to play, relax[6] and, perhaps, even organise.

Baker, K. (2009, 24 March). Absenteeism and stress loads up as recession hits work-life balance. *Personnel Today.* Retrieved 12 September 2009 from http://www.personneltoday.com/articles/2009/03/24/49980/absenteeism-and-stress-loads-up-as-recession-hits-work-life.html.

Burke, R. J. & Cooper, C. L. (Eds.) (2008). *The Long Work Hours Culture: Causes, Consequences and Choices.* Bingley: Emerald Group.

The Chartered Institute for Personnel and Development (2009, April). Working hours in the UK. Retrieved 12 September 2009 from http://www.cipd.co.uk/subjects/hrpract/hoursandholidays/ukworkhrs. Quoting: Chartered Institute of Personnel and Development (2003). Living to work? *Survey report.* London: CIPD.

Clougherty, T. (2009, January). How to promote the free market in 2009. Retrieved 12 September 2009 from http://www.adamsmith.org/think-piece/economy/how-to-promote-the-free-market-in-2009-200901122748.

Diederichsen, D. (2008). On [surplus] value in art. *Reflections 01.* Rotterdam: Witte de With Publishers, Sternberg Press.

Heartfield, J. (2008). Creativity as ideology. *Renewal,* 16(2), pp. 28-34.

Hofmeyr, B. (2008). Save money. Live better? In B. Hofmeyr (Ed.). *The Wal-Mart Phenomenon. Resisting Neo-Liberal Power Through Art, Design and Theory.* Maastricht: Jan Van Eyck Publishers. pp. 11-30.

Kinman, G. (2009, 5 March). The long work hours culture: Our hard days' nights explored. *Times Higher Education,* Retrieved 12 September 2009 from http://www.timeshighereducation.co.uk/story.sp?storyCode=405651&sectioncode=26.

Vishmidt, M. (2007). It was the market that did it: (dilatory account - decisive action - dissipative tendency). In *Producta50* (pp. 284-292), Barcelona: Yproductions. Retrieved 12 September 2009 from http://ypsite.net/pdfs/productaang.pdf.

Woods, D. (2009, 18 June). Unpaid overtime is increasingly common among UK employees. *Human Resources Magazine.* Retrieved 12 September 2009 from http://www.hrmagazine.co.uk/news/914188/Unpaid-overtime-increasingly-common-among-UK-employees.

Trades Union Congress (2009, 8 January). Unpaid overtime in 2008: A record year for long hours. Retrieved 12 September 2009 from http://www.worksmart.org.uk/news/2009/01/unpaid-overtime-in-2008-a-record-year-for-long-hours/trackback.

AGAINST PLEASURE. AGAIN
THE WORK OF ART OR A DIALECTIC OF EMANCIPATION[1].

JIM COLQUHOUN

QUESTION: CAN ONE LIVE WITHOUT WORKING?

ANSWER: WE CAN ONLY LIVE WITHOUT WORKING. WE ONLY WORK
THROUGH NECESSITY, TO SURVIVE. LIFE STARTS WHEN ONE STOPS WORKING.
WORK IS INCOMPATIBLE WITH LIFE WHICH IS ESSENTIALLY CREATIVE. LIFE
IS A PERMANENT INVENTION, SURVIVAL IS NOTHING BUT A MONOTONOUS
WORK OF REPRODUCTION.
(Vaneigem, 2005, p. 82).

In our rationalised and bureaucratic society the idea of 'work' is the cornerstone of our belief in a progressive moral order. We give ourselves over to 'alienated' labour because it is the correct thing to do in that the alternative is the slide into moral turpitude. Under the sign of 'work' we give our time willingly and our ability to question this state of affairs is curtailed because we can see no alternative to economic servitude. At heart, this formulation is designed to instil the idea that we are better off being told what we must do. Rather than a pleasurable and creative engagement with the world, we are encouraged to 'deny' our desires, or at least to 'save them up' for some notional time when we will be allowed to 'indulge ourselves', although this time may be put off indefinitely.

1. This text is extracted from a much more wide-ranging reflection on the ethics of work and of art.

One route out of this impasse is to designate oneself 'artist'. Here, one is encouraged to think, the ordinary rules simply do not apply. It is implied that we can escape the strictures of the capitalist mode of production by 'regressing' to a state analogous to childhood, in that we are allowed to 'play' beyond the strict demarcations of the capitalist hegemony. This perhaps romantic and illusory notion is fostered to encourage the idea that a limited 'escape' may still be possible. It is a powerful idea, mitigated only by the undoubted poverty and alienation experienced by many of those attempting to scrape a living in this field. In becoming artists we are attempting to negate this work/play dichotomy. In other words, we are disputing the separation inherent in the division of labour. Work and play become indivisible because they are one and the same.

But in the early twenty-first century, the division between our 'professional' lives and our personal lives has become ever more blurred, helped along by

ST LIFE.

the ubiquity of communications technology, but also through the demands of changing work patterns. For many of us, 'clocking off' is no longer an option as work life bleeds into home life to the point where we are never actually *off* in any real sense. Yet, in spite of this dire prognosis, art-making or creativity of any kind is still, arguably, the prime site of 'unalienated' labour. Even if the products of artistic endeavour are routinely reified and co-opted by markets, the actual producers of said artefacts/ideas seem to escape this process through complete control of their own labour. This antinomianism in the face of the (presumed) ascendancy of global capitalism is hotly contested, not least by Marxists and other leftists, and the idea that it may be possible to escape, even momentarily, the totalising effects of the market is taken as a sign of heresy. But perhaps art can, in fact, be said to dialectically oppose the strictures imposed on the majority? Marx himself said as much: "…capitalist production is hostile to certain branches of spiritual production, for example, art and poetry" (1969, p. 285).

Of course, it can be argued that commodification can and does determine the outcomes of an art-practice. Many artists undoubtedly create their works specifically for a particular niche, or may, perhaps unconsciously, follow a trend that has proven financially viable. Or indeed, powerful artists, gallerists, and other cultural commissars may 'massage' the sector to their own benefit. But let's assume that there are many practitioners out there who routinely produce work that is by its very nature – a collective venture, an impermanent site-specific work, or a time-based performance – less likely to be reified as the luxury commodity 'art' and therefore produce profit. This is a delicate balancing act. Where and when do you draw the line? What is an acceptable career move and what is not? How to refuse? Many artists have sought to escape from the perceived strictures of markets and institutions by recourse to strategies that, at least initially, are unrecuperable. This denial of the trajectory of a professional art career is a risky business, but was seen as preferable to an outright capitulation to market values.

> Perhaps the original ethos of Conceptual art and Fluxus, their way of relating art to life, was actually quite close to this spirit. After all, it was also about realising that you could just write a sentence on a wall or meet friends and improvise something, and that would be enough: you could be finished for the day (!), so you could relax, go out and live your life . . . you could still create a conceptual gesture at any time and it would be art: you would be an artist and you would lack nothing. Whatever happened to this ethos of anti-professionalism? (Verwoert, 2009, para. 7).

Emblematic of this attempt to escape commodification is the willingness of artists to 'de-skill'. Often this has meant delegating the work of construction, or adopting an explicitly 'managerial' approach to resources. Throughout the 1960s and into the '70s, artists self-consciously adopted the mien and even the dress codes of both manual labourers and white-collar workers, even going so far as to ape their working day. I'm thinking here of Frank Stella's adoption of a 'blue-collar' persona, or Gilbert and George's anachronistic (at the time) return to a kind of buttoned-up 'Englishness'. Some artists, such as Jannis Kounellis and Adrian Piper, gave up making art altogether[2] in an attempt to escape commodification. Robert Morris' *Box with the Sound of its own Making* (1961) neatly encapsulates the flavour of a period that tried to erase the bourgeois category 'art' altogether by conflating it with the category 'work'. The *éminence grise* is of course Marcel Duchamp, his 'escape' from the category 'artist'[3] seemingly complete. Critic and curator Helen Molesworth (2003) argues that

2. At least for a time.

3. Whilst still secretly working on *Etant Donnés.*

4. And, a direct attack on the idea of the artist as elevated 'genius' hovering in some rarified plane, somewhere above the common herd.

> A historical convergence had occurred. Just as artists relinquished traditional artistic skills and the production of discrete art objects, the status of labour and the production of goods in the culture at large were also changing profoundly as the American industrial economy, based in manufacturing, shifted to a post-industrial economy rooted in managerial and service labour (p. 25).

The very terminology used in the art world is that of capitalist production and commodification. We make 'artworks'. We have a 'practice' much as a dentist or a lawyer. We have implicitly placed ourselves within the category 'professional' by using this technical language of the 'professions'. Yet, an escape mode has long been formulated. Duchamp's *readymades* had thrown the whole notion of the artist as faithful reproducer and elevated *savant* into disarray by introducing the playful notion that *ideas* themselves could become the work, or that mass-produced objects could be transformed into 'art' simply by being designated as such by an 'artist'. All of this, of course, a direct challenge to the concept of artistic labour[4] and a break from the past, the reverberations of which would be felt for decades. Although an unfortunate side effect of this categorical disjuncture has been that much of the 'public' have been left adrift, struggling to come to terms with an art that is radically *other*, it has meant that the field of artistic possibilities has expanded exponentially.

ESCAPE VELOCITY

> One of modernism's many promises was that art offered possible resistance to an increasingly regimented life under the auspices of industrialisation. From the arts and crafts

movement to the Bauhaus, the history of modern art is shot through with the dream of an integration of the realms of art and life, work and leisure, such that the alienation produced by the fragmented nature of modern labour would be ameliorated (Molesworth, 2003, p. 26).

The recent history of art is littered with attempts, both individually and collectively to escape from the market, negating it and critiquing it in the process. These attempts to escape the gallery system, the museological 'capture' of art, and the reification of 'revolt' were, in part, engendered by the critique offered by Herbert Marcuse in his book *Eros and Civilisation*[5]. In his treatise, Marcuse hoped to show that the dialectic of productivity, consumption, and destruction inherent in the capitalist mode of production could be negated by the 'post-scarcity economy', and that the perceived need to 'toil' endlessly on a production line would, due to technological advances, become a thing of the past. In essence, Marcuse was proposing an economy of 'leisure', a new and startling 'reality principle' based on the liberating potential of technology. Exploitation would be forgone by a society that based social relations on a 'pleasure principle' rather than a 'reality principle'.

This was his specifically 'neo-Freudian' formulation, in that Freud's pessimism regarding human potential is taken as an idea to be superseded. Freud proposed that, initially, man lives only for immediate gratification until this primal urge is ameliorated by the realisation that this constant striving for pleasure is doomed to disappointment. This gloomy realisation leads him to 'renunciation and restraint', which, according to Freud 'safeguards' or modifies the pleasure principle by allowing it to be deferred. Marcuse, however, points out that the unconscious retains the pleasure principle in its unfettered imaginative potentiality and that it has a profound effect on social relations. He sees this 'return of the repressed' as the hidden history of civilisation; the 'illogical' motor driving behaviour deemed unacceptable by a supposedly rational society.

5. As well as: Marcuse, H. (1964). *One-Dimensional Man: Studies in the Ideology of Advanced Industrial Society.* Boston: Beacon.

Repression is arrived at, not just through some sublimated unconscious process, but through the ways in which our civilisation is in thrall to a particularly instrumental, productive, and teleological view of human progress. It is akin to a self-fulfilling prophecy, in that it is the inequalities inherent in social relations that are reproduced within the psyche of the individual in a closed loop of ideological cathexis. In other words, we allow ourselves to be bullied into selling our time to a system that values us, more often than not, as commodities rather than as people, as units that can be picked up and discarded on a managerial whim. Artists and other 'creatives' can be said to be the exemplars of this idea, in that they willingly embrace 'precarity' and the ability to 'move' with the flows and eddies of capital.

THE GAME OF ART

> We need the chaos, the surprise, the dystopianism and utopianism of art more than ever, to propel us towards a play-dominant rather than a work-dominant world. We need a vibrant art and culture in the information age because it points us to the necessary space in a system, network or field where movement and change can always happen (Kane, 2004, p. 231).

Aware of the contradictions, artists are attempting to work within *and* against a hyper-saturated mediascape, happy to get away with working the edges whilst pulling a fast one on the state providers of funds and part-time employment. While it is true that artists can seem to encapsulate the perfectly deregulated, singularized and ectogenous 'affiliate' demanded by modern employers – the 'creative classes', as defined by Richard Florida – they are also as often playfully challenging their own status as 'professionals' by forming a congeries of ever-shifting grouplets, fly-by-night organisations, or peripatetic gallery spaces[6] in an attempt to circumvent or distort the perceived career trajectory of the successful artist[7].

6. Often all at once!

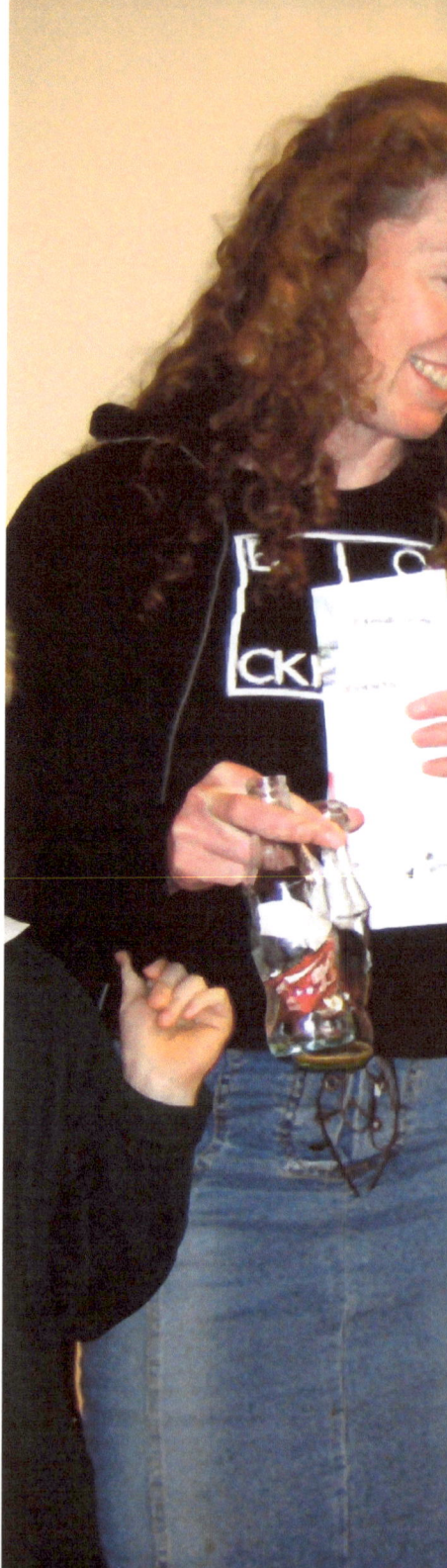

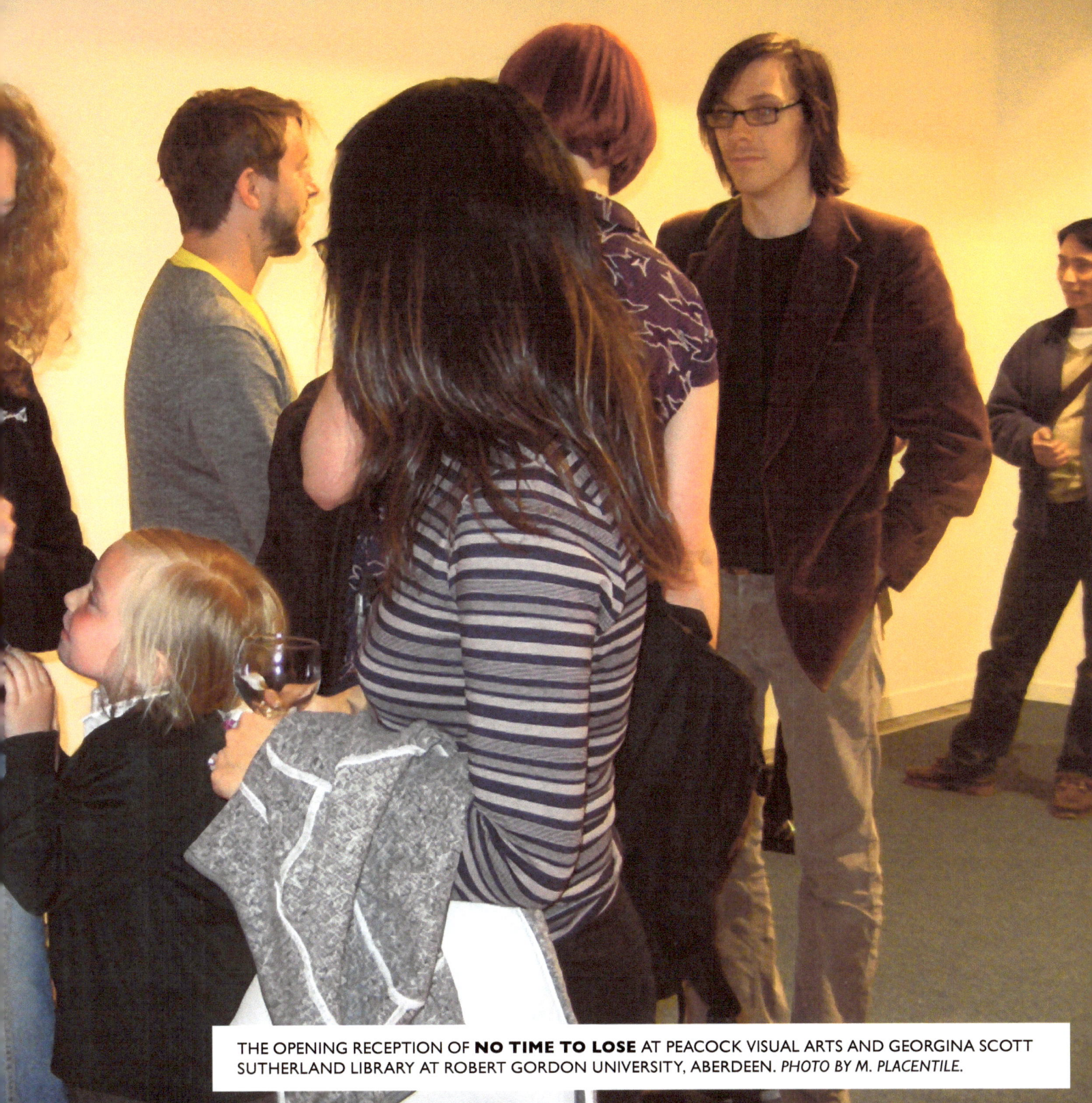

THE OPENING RECEPTION OF **NO TIME TO LOSE** AT PEACOCK VISUAL ARTS AND GEORGINA SCOTT SUTHERLAND LIBRARY AT ROBERT GORDON UNIVERSITY, ABERDEEN. *PHOTO BY M. PLACENTILE.*

That all of this flies in the face of New Labour's dream of a somnolent, workerist, and business-friendly paradise may come as no surprise. Prime Minister Gordon Brown's much-touted 'work ethic' is at one and the same time a cynical, vote-grabbing love letter to the ever-striving middle-classes and a strict admonition to 'the idle' that their heinous misuse of their time will shortly be curtailed. That those in this position might actually be thriving (if poor) is anathema. That they might actually choose to play – with drugs, with technology, with communitarian forms, the permissible, and themselves – is an unacceptable response. Yet, in the face of mounting insecurity and looming financial meltdown, it may be the only course open to many of us. Enforced idleness could be viewed as a boon. Instead of rigid adherence to a puritanical, doctrinaire, and machinic ideology we could become open to the manifold potentialities of a society unconstrained.

7. Although as often as not these can be viewed as attempts to raise one's profile in a sector teeming with fellow wannabes.

What strikes me is the fact that, in our society, art has become something that is related only to objects and not to individuals or to life. That art is something that is specialized or done by experts who are artists. But couldn't everyone's life become a work of art? Why should the lamp or the house be an art object but not our life? (Foucault, 1997, p. 262).

In *The Accursed Share* (1991), George Bataille discusses Marxism in terms of the desire to free the world from this tyranny of *things* (i.e. from 'the economy') and, in terms of the proposition, that it is in abandoning this world of things that we might liberate ourselves from our enslavement to them. As Bataille goes on to point out, capitalism, on the other hand, is a surrender *to* things: 'heedless to the consequences and seeing nothing beyond them' (Bataille, Volume 1, p. 136) and has therefore usurped the future as being an infinite progression towards a limitless proliferation of stuff. In so doing it has inaugurated a system of psychic regimentation that subordinates desire to the reproduction of a manufactured and artificially stimulated ossature. Our ability to think beyond the precepts of a system that *encloses* desire within an armature of intense commodification may be possible only if we look again at our relationship with, to use Johan Huizinga's term, the *play factor* and, in the process, negate the binary antithesis of play and seriousness, work and non-work.

Bataille, G. (1991). *The Accursed Share*. (R. J. Hurley, Trans.). New York: Zone Books.

Florida, R. (2002). *The Rise of the Creative Class: And how it's Transforming Work, Leisure, Community and Everyday life*. New York: Perseus Book Group.

Foucault, M. (1997). *Ethics, Subjectivity and Truth*. (P. Rabinow, Ed.). (R. J. Hurley, Trans.). New York: The New Press.

Huizinga, J. (1955). *Homo Ludens; A Study of the Play-Element in Culture*. Boston: Beacon Press.

(2005, Spring). In conversation with Raoul Vaneigem. *The Idler*, 35, pp. 80-87.

Kane, P. (2004). *The Play Ethic: A Manifesto for a Different way of Living. London*: Macmillan.

Marcuse, H. (1955). *Eros and Civilization*. Boston: Beacon.

Marx, K. (1969). Theories of surplus-value. In *Capital*. (E. Burns, Trans.). London: Lawrence & Wishardt (Original work published 1863).

Molesworth, M. & The Baltimore Museum of Art (2003). Work ethic. In H. Molesworth (Ed.), *Work Ethic*: exhibition catalogue, 12 October 2003 - 4 January 2004. University Park, Pennsylvania The Pennsylvania State University Press. pp. 25-51.

Verwoert, J. (2009, March). Life work. *Frieze*, 121, Retrieved 12 September 2009 from http://www.frieze.com/issue/article/life_work.

TOO MUCH, TOO LITTLE
CONNECTING JOBLESSNESS AND OVERWORK

TORU YAMAMORI

OH, WHY DO YOU WORK EIGHT HOURS OR MORE?
THERE'D BE JOBS FOR US ALL IF YOU'D ONLY WORK FOUR.

(Hallelujah, I'm a Bum, by Harry McClintock et al., 2005)

Many visionary thinkers anticipated that society would eventually require fewer working hours as a result of technological advances. In the nineteenth century, Karl Marx suggested that machinery would decrease the time needed for labour (1973, pp. 690-712), and in the mid-twentieth century, the Canadian-American economist John Kenneth Galbraith pointed out that technological innovation was decreasing the working hours needed to maintain society, and proposed severing the relationship between labour and income. Among those who were not specifically economists, the English philosopher Bertrand Russell stated that four hours of labour should be enough to fulfil society's needs (2006, p. 87). Since the 1960s, critical thinkers such as Austrian and French social philosopher and journalist, Andre Gorz, German political sociologist Claus Offe, Belgian political philosopher, Phillipe van Parijs, and Italian sociologist and political philosopher, Antonio Negri, predicted a future with less time spent working; however, in reality everywhere one looks, long working hours are unevenly distributed, or more accurately, long working hours exist in tandem with unemployment. Why is it that many people suffer from excessive working hours on one hand while, on the other, many suffer from unemployment? One reason must be that there is no fair distribution of labour.

DREAMS OF WORK-SHARING

Advocates of work-sharing have promoted fair labour distribution since the 1980s, yet there has not been any significant progress. A major reason for this is that permanent employees are reluctant to accept lower wages as a result of working fewer hours while management will not accept decreased working hours without lowering wages. One solution to this stalemate might be for the State to step in and compensate workers for the fraction of wages lost due to decreased hours. France's Green Party calls their proposal in this vein, "The Second Check." One could also call it a partial implementation of "basic income".

Basic income is an unconditional guaranteed income for all. Van Parijs (1995), defines it as "an income paid by the government to each full member of society (1) even if she is not willing to work, (2) irrespective of her being rich or poor, (3) whoever she lives with, and (4) no matter which part of the country she lives in" (p. 35). He deliberately avoids setting a basic income level, but basic income proposals are usually based on the notion that it should cover the costs of a decent standard of living. The "Second Check" is, therefore, a partial basic income solution because it pays only for wages lost due to reduced working hours. Going a step further, some propose, as an alternative to wages, basic income as a new form of income distribution for a society that would require fewer working hours. In addition to van Parijs, German drug store chain owner Götz Werner (2006) is another notable advocate of the basic income model; however, such points of view remain in the minority.

PERSONALIZING THE ISSUES

Lacking political will to change the distribution of working hours through policies or other legislation, various European countries and Japan focus on "work/life balance" as an issue rather than "work sharing". Work sharing is, first and foremost, a matter of labour distribution (that is, of creating full employment and shorter working hours involving progress measured by macro-economic indicators) while work/life balance compartmentalizes the problem at the level of individual workers and their employers. Work/life balance is presented as a personal issue for individual workers with regard to how they divide their time between labour and activities outside the workplace, such as leisure or housework. Thus, the problem of overwork is relegated to each employer's ability to provide a flexible working environment. This obviously shifts the focus from the macro level to the micro level, and the assessment of work/life balance policies is, in fact, completely severed from unemployment indicators and the unequal distribution of work among the population[1].

1. In order to relate work/life balance progress to observable macro indicators birth rates trump unemployment figures. The terms for work/life balance in America, "Work-Family Balance," and Germany, "family friendly," express this concept quite well.

In the UK, work/life balance policies began in 2000 under New Labour and are, in fact, proposing "flexible working". According to British social policy analyst, Hartley Dean, "flexibility for high-paid core workers is to do with skills: they must be able to continually adapt and retrain. Flexibility for low-paid peripheral workers is to do with time: they must accommodate themselves to efficient working patterns and the fluctuating demands of the market" (2007, p. 271). Thus, unemployment and flexibility are not mutually exclusive for low wage workers. Rather, for these workers, the logical outcome of work/life balance is unemployment or under-employment. For highly paid workers, if 'flexibility' means ceaselessly meeting ever-changing demands for new skills, as Dean suggests, the required long hours of training and work mean an inability to allocate time for leisure or family. If work/life balance policies amount, as they do in the UK, to furthering the flexibility of workers, they further the co-existence of long-hours of working and training for some, and unemployment and under-employment for others.

IMMATERIAL LABOUR: A NEW PARADIGM?

"Flexibility of work" policies sustain the coexistence of overwork and unemployment and should be discontinued. Traditional workers would be protected if deregulation policies were abandoned in favour of the restoration of social legislation such as that gained during the welfare state period, or strict adherence to 'equal pay for equal work' (as is the case in the Netherlands), or both in tandem. It's counterintuitive, but discontinuing current UK-style work/life balance policies and returning to previous systems would bring us far closer to achieving *genuine* work/life balance.

However, considering the transformation of working conditions particularly for those engaged in what is commonly called 'immaterial labour', a genuine work/life balance for all workers cannot be achieved by instituting social regulations. The hegemony of immaterial labour changes the very conditions of work. To begin with, the forms of labour associated with professions covered under this term require flexibility in order to function, and traditional regulations couldn't reconcile the emotional involvement required by people to do their jobs, or the unavoidable blurring of work and leisure

time that inevitably results. In the industrial paradigm, workers produced almost exclusively during the hours in the factory; however, when production means solving a problem, or formulating an idea, or creating a relationship, work time has the potential to extend over the entire scope of life. As Hardt and Negri rightly point out, ideas or images come to mind not only in the office, but also while showering or dreaming (2004, pp. 111-112). As work spreads into every waking (and perhaps even sleeping, or dreaming) moment, workers are unable to avoid involvement while, at the same time, the actual conditions of exploitation escape any effort to regulate measurable working hours. Thus, in order to foster true work/life balance, we will need more than a dispensation of existing rhetoric and renewed regulations from the past; we will need a whole new way of looking at the place of work in our lives.

Translated by Brian Small; edited by M. Placentile.

Dean, H. (2007). Poor parent? The realities of work-life balance in a low-income neighbourhood, *Benefits: A Journal of Poverty and Social Justice*, 15 (3). pp. 271-282.

Hardt, M. & Negri, A. (2004). *Multitude: War and Democracy in the Age of Empire*. New York: Penguin.

Marx, K. (1973). Fragments on machinery. In Grundrisse: *Foundations of the Critique of Political Economy*. (M. Nicolaus, Trans.). London: Penguin. (Original work written 1857-61, published 1953).

McClintock, H., "Haywire Mac", et. al. (2005). Hallelujah, I'm a bum. In *The Little Red Songbook*. Philadelphia: Industrial Workers of the World (Original work published 1909).

Russell, B. (2006). *Roads to Freedom*. Nottingham: Spokesman. (Original work published 1918).

Van Parijs, P. (1995). *Real Freedom for all: What (if Anything) can Justify Capitalism?* Oxford: Oxford University Press.

Werner, G. W. (2006). *Ein Grund für die Zukunft: das Grundeinkommen*. Interviews und reaktionen. Stuttgart: Freies Geistesleben.

NO TIME TO LOSE

MILENA PLACENTILE

FRAMING IDEOLOGIES

Economic systems are ideological structures that assert particular world views and related values. Much like systems of religion, economic systems tend to be pursued with great zeal and are often declared the foundations upon which society and its institutions are best structured. As such, these systems are conceived to permeate all aspects of daily life: home, school, work, and leisure. When the chief advocates of a particular system stand to gain through a steadfast adherence to that system, they present it as the sole possibility or, at least, the possibility that is most rational and/or "true".

The Chicago School of Economics, made globally dominant by arguably the most influential American economist of the twentieth century, Milton Friedman, is predicated on an unwavering faith in what is widely known as neoliberalism. In most basic terms, proponents of neoliberalism advocate that markets ought to be free from government intervention of any kind, and any failure of the system is attributed not to a flaw in the system itself, but to an external force that prohibited the market from operating without restraint.

In her highly-acclaimed book *The Shock Doctrine*, Canadian journalist and activist Naomi Klein (2007) writes:

> Like all fundamentalist faiths, Chicago school economics is, for its true believers, a closed

loop. The starting premise is that the free market is a perfect scientific system, one in which individuals, acting on their own self-interested desires, create the maximum benefits for all. It follows ineluctably that if something is working within the free market economy – high inflation or soaring unemployment – it has to be because the market is not truly free. There must be some interference, some distortion in the system. The Chicago school is always the same: a stricter and more complete application of the fundamentals (p. 59).

American Professor of history and political economy of communication, Robert W. McChesney, makes a similar assertion in his essay *Noam Chomsky and the Struggle Against Neoliberalism* (1999):

> The ultimate trump card for the defenders of neoliberalism, however, is that there is no alternative. Communist societies, social democracies, and even modest social welfare states like the United States have all failed, the neoliberals proclaim, and their citizens have accepted neoliberalism as the only feasible course. It may well be imperfect, but it is the only economic system possible (para. 4).

The notion that the new economy must be accepted was insistently asserted by former British Prime Minister Margaret Thatcher to the extent that "there is no alternative" is so widely associated with her that it may well have been her personal mantra[1].

Award-winning Canadian scientist, environmentalist, and broadcaster, David Suzuki, is among those who identify economic systems as human inventions that have been irrationally elevated in significance. Commenting on how fixations with the dominant model of economics can be linked to the causes of widespread ecological damage, he writes:

> We act as if the economy is some kind of natural force that we must all placate or serve in every way possible. But wait! Some things, like gravity, the speed of light, entropy, and the first and second laws of thermodynamics, are forces of nature. There's nothing we can do about them except live within the boundaries they delimit.
>
> But the economy, the market, currency – we created these entities, and if they don't work, we should look beyond trying to get them back up and running the way they were. We should fix them or toss them out and replace them (Suzuki with Moola, F., 2009, para. 5-6).

In recent years those destructive forces of capitalism have, yet again, begun to reveal themselves quite transparently. From corporate bailouts of obsolete, environmentally harmful sectors using public money, to CEOs receiving astronomical bonuses despite corporate losses, to increased unemployment while the cost of living soars, one would imagine it a good time to rethink the structures through which we circulate goods and services. This, however, has not been the case since those who benefit from this world order – "extremely wealthy investors and less than one thousand large corporations" (McChesney, 1999, para. 1) – stand to lose a great deal (Chomsky, 2003, p. 60).

To shape the world they desire, this elite of free market "believers" has defined a powerful hierarchy, where policy makers affiliated with the International Monetary Fund, World Bank, and numerous Central Banks dictate a course for all others to follow (Klein, 2007). Superstar CEOs – the more cutthroat the better – become models of professional excellence and are rewarded celebrity status and income. Meanwhile, struggling workers, from part-time burger flippers to PDA-wielding management types, cling to the hope of achieving their own, individual financial salvation. It's difficult to understand and

1. Eighty-seven speeches delivered by Thatcher containing the phrase "there is no alternative" could be found online at margaretthatcher.org as of 28 August 2009.

recognize the machinations influencing the big picture from the isolated position of a single being lost within the mess.

As shown by Luc Boltanski and Eve Chiapello (2005, pp. 243-251, 273-314) and Chernomas and Hudson (2007), this "new economy" never promised a win/win situation. Rather, it is predicated on the systematic dismantling of workers' rights in order to achieve profits for those closest to the top. Labour is attacked from all angles: through corporate downsizing, tax cuts, anti-labour legislation, and reduced social spending. Years of high unemployment in Canada, Europe, and the United States have progressively worsened through free trade agreements that allow capital to flow freely toward cheaper labour supplied in nations where workers have even fewer rights and protections.

According to the neoliberal ideology, however, any actual inequities and their results are not systemic problems, but individual failings, because the market supposedly allows perfect conditions for us all to succeed. The values of this economic belief filter their way into the mindset of workers via the concept of a solid work ethic. Those who keep busy will be rewarded, not in the form of a decent wage, job security, or health benefits today, but in an "afterlife" made comfortable thanks to retirement packages enabled through investment in companies that —

through the hard work of employees — can and will reach unprecedented levels of profitability (McChesney, 1999; Chernomas & Hudson, 2007, pp. 22-36).

Trish Hennessy and Armine Yalnizyan (2009) report on the disconnect between the promise that smarter, harder work, and less reliance on the government would trickle down wealth to all citizens, and the actual outcomes of free-market policies:

> The lion's share of Canada's economic growth went to the richest 10% which started to break away from the rest of us. Over the past generation the share of incomes going to the richest 1% soared, but most Canadian families had to settle for a smaller share of income. All Canadian families, except for the richest 10%, were putting in more hours a week into the workplace. Two hundred hours more compared to just 10 years ago. But incomes didn't grow for the majority (np.).

Chernomas and Hudson (2007, p. 30) relay similarly disparaging figures about the United States, and growing inequity is evident in statistics from around the world. In 2005, BBC News conveyed details of a UN report noting that "the world is more unequal today than it was 10 years ago, despite considerable economic growth in many regions" (Price, np.).

Those of us who still have jobs are well aware that fewer colleagues means longer, harder hours, but for less compensation regardless of increasing costs of living (Boltanski & Chiapello, p. 249-250). Caught in an isolating flurry of overwork and stress, who has time to notice this is affecting not only individual life, but collective life, as well? And now, facing the most widely recognized international economic crisis since the Great Depression of the 1930s, people are beginning to wonder if the dominant neoliberal ideologies of the past thirty years have just been a great big lie (Chernomas & Hudson, 2007; Klein, 2007). Our employers might be clocking in record profits, but caught in our own financial binds, how could we dare complain?

FRAMING RESISTANCE

Neoliberalism declares that if we don't like something, we can "vote with our feet" by, for example, opting out of poorly paid or overly labourious work (Chernomas & Hudson, 2007, pp. 48-74), yet anyone who needs employment knows such advice comes from an oversimplified, if not somewhat disconnected, reading of reality. What we can do, however, is re-direct our energies to transform our world through collective action and collectively applied pressure.

The task of revealing and dismantling the neoliberal economic order is vast, and it does not help that people the world over are losing confidence in the capacity for the electoral process to represent their interests and promote genuine change. The problems we as workers face are not insurmountable and sharing information about our struggles, ideas, and efforts is vital to increasing critical knowledge and coordinating acts of resistance.

What we observe around us daily serves as important points of entry into discussions about social and political reality. Many people, including those who are under- and unemployed, find themselves boxed into frantic states of being due to an overall faster pace of life made worse by growing economic pressure (Menzies, 2005; Honoré, 2005). Boltanski and Chiapello (2005, p. 151-156) specifically articulate how what they call 'the new spirit of capitalism' has affected not only how we think about money and possessions, but also how we perceive work and employment. This means we are all inculcated into the structures of neoliberalism, yet we have motivations to seek alternate possibilities.

How can we assess our personal circumstances, recognize them in light of the circumstances of others, achieve solidarity across the artificial gaps that have been gouged, and redirect our efforts toward the creation of a world that is more equitable, sustainable, compassionate, and fair? Overwork keeps us isolated and occupied. Thus, it seems one of the first things we must realize is that the circumstances imposing overwork are not accidental, and that none of us are alone.

Models of work that privilege commitment to one's job over personal care have gone too far. The negative effects are widespread, including health and relationship problems, accidents caused by cutting corners or fatigue, and social and political turmoil caused by decreased civic involvement. Various European countries are striving to establish more humane policies, but there are still many sectors operating at unsustainable and unhealthy levels. Beyond that, the challenge to switch has been great, particularly in the face of economic pressures caused by globalization, and now recession. Activists, health care professionals, and other concerned citizens are making progress, but there are still numerous discussions to have and changes to make. How can we stop living for the economy and by the clock and start living in ways that are more gratifying and equitable?

No Time to Lose was a response to the systemic decline of personal time experienced by people worldwide due to increased hours spent working. Bringing together artists from countries affected by the phenomenon of overwork through an exhibition and program of events, it drew attention to the unsustainability of social and economic systems that do not afford people sufficient time outside of work. It also addressed the individual and civic costs associated with insufficient time to attend to personal and community life. Envisioned as a contribution to global efforts directed at motivating and mobilizing people to trust their instincts and take back their time, No Time to Lose featured artwork that encouraged audiences to disengage from their stressful routines and consider what they are losing due to unbalanced lifestyles.

Most importantly, the exhibition sought to remind people that they are not alone in this struggle and encouraged the view that, together, we can make changes for the better. By inviting audiences to consider what they were giving up due to overwork, and to decide whether the economic system facilitating overwork offered enough in return, the exhibition also revealed ways society encourages overwork, such as through the availability of wireless technology, and personal care products that offer "24-hour action." Hoping to empower audiences, featured projects sought to demonstrate how small actions can create ripples to encourage further actions. For example, if we humanize our workplace by addressing each other as full and complete people with personal lives, and not merely as "co-workers," what else might be possible?

Aiming to involve as wide a range of people as possible, gallery visitors were actively encouraged to explore and share thoughts, while unsuspecting individuals were offered opportunities to engage with unexpected ideas in public space through interventions deployed outdoors. All of the featured artworks welcomed viewers to draw on their personal experiences to extrapolate meaning from each project and consider that, no matter how isolated they might feel from other human beings through the course of their work, we are all in this together. We can find ways of reclaiming personal time and restoring the balance we need to collectively achieve new and humane social practices.

No Time to Lose did not purport to offer specific solutions for immediate change; rather the gentle reminder that our current reality is not the only option, and that if change is what we want and need, we must consider how our daily actions support an unhealthy and unjust system. The artists featured in the exhibition ask questions about how we define time and space and how we relate to one another within those definitions. These are questions that prompt us to think about our everyday realities and to think about the subtle changes that can amass into larger, transformative movements comprised of people joining together to resist inequality.

Boltanski, L. & Chiapello, E. (2005). *The New Spirit of Capitalism*. London: Verso.

Chernomas, R. & Hudson, I. (2007). *Social Murder and Other Shortcomings of Conservative Economics*. Winnipeg: Arbeiter Ring Publishing.

Hennessy, T. & Yalnizyan, A. (2009, 31 July). Canada's growing gap explained. *Canadian Centre for Policy Alternatives*. Video posted to http://www.policyalternatives. ca/reports/2009/07/reports studies2272/?pa=BB736455. Retrieved 28 August 2009.

Honoré, C. (2005). *In praise of slow: How a Worldwide Movement is Challenging the Cult of Speed*. Toronto: Vintage Canada.

Klein, N. (2007). *The shock doctrine: The rRse of Disaster Capitalism* Toronto: Random House of Canada Limited.

McChesney, R. W. (1999, 1 April). Noam Chomsky and the struggle against neoliberalism. *Monthly Review*. Retrieved 28 August 2009 from http://www.chomsky.info/onchomsky/19990401.htm.

Menzies, H. (2005). *Not Enough Time: Stress and the Crisis of Modern Life*. Toronto: Douglas & McIntyre.

Price, S. (2005, 25 August). UN finds global inequality rising. *BBC News*. Retrieved 22 August 2009 from http://news.bbc.co.uk/2/hi/americas/4185458.stm.

Suzuki, D. & Moola, F. (2009, 21 August). It's time for a new economic paradigm. *Science Matters*. Retrieved 22 August 2009 from http://www.davidsuzuki.org/about_us/Dr_David_Suzuki/Article_Archives/weekly08190901.asp.

NO TIME TO LOSE AT PEAC

MILENA PLACENTILE

SAKI SATOM, *DESK PROJECT*, 2005-2008, FOUR-CHANNEL VIDEO INSTALLATION (APPROXIMATELY 6 MINUTES EACH).

Saki Satom is a Japanese performance and video artist who produces work motivated by her interest in conventionally accepted behaviours and interpersonal exchanges in the context of public space. Seeking to foster a participatory aspect to her experimental scenarios, Satom's *Desk Project* invited visitors to perform the socially subversive act of crawling under a desk. In fact, this was the only way viewers could watch her videos, which featured the artist interviewing four professionals (i.e. a teacher of etiquette and a cultural attaché) about Western style greetings.

Displaying the videos underneath office desks allowed Satom to comment on workplace formalities. Many individuals spend extended and exhausting periods at their desks and, even though employers must permit breaks by law, many employees worry about being considered lazy or unmotivated if they don't push themselves as hard as they can. As a considerate nod to individual vulnerability, Satom offered the child-like action of crawling under furniture as a means of fulfilling the occasional need to escape. Her focus on the subject of etiquette within her installation reminiscent of a workplace can furthermore be read as a suggestion that better interpersonal skills can

offer a humanizing influence, thereby reinforcing the need for employees to be treated like people, not machines. What further benefits can greater empathy bring?

ANJA HERTENBERGER & ANJA STEIDINGER, *ROAM/STRAY*, 2007-2008, MULTIMEDIA INSTALLATION (AUDIO COMPONENT APPROXIMATELY 6 MINUTES).

ANJA HERTENBERGER & ANJA STEIDINGER, *WORKPLACES AT NIGHT*, 2006-2008, TWO-CHANNEL VIDEO INSTALLATION WITH PHOTOGRAPHIC AND SCULPTURAL COMPONENTS (VIDEOS APPROXIMATELY 16 MINUTES AND 20 MINUTES EACH).

Anja Hertenberger (Germany/Netherlands) & Anja Steidinger (Germany/Spain) develop collaborative, process-based projects as a way of linking their friendship into their artistic endeavours, thereby transcending professional relationships based solely on work and productivity.

For *No Time to Lose*, the artists proposed two performance-based investigations, the collected material from which would generate the content for two installations. They initially sought to conduct actions that visualized connections between the experiences of individuals as "workers" and as "human beings" by drawing attention to the complex nature of everyday life and by exploring the extent to which work creeps into personal time, and vice versa. However, over the course of the two-year period leading up to the presentation of these projects, their research, discussions, trial actions, and feedback sessions led them to think about the changing appearance of work from something that is primarily production-based to something that is increasingly immaterial (i.e. administration). This lack of visible output, they believe, is one of the reasons work has become depoliticized over time, even in the minds of workers themselves.

Roam/Stray was a project realized over the space of three cities: Amsterdam, Barcelona, and finally Aberdeen. Visiting one another in their respective home cities prior to the exhibition, Hertenberger and Steidinger spent time traveling on public transport to observe and interact with fellow passengers, particularly those who appear stressed out, or who appeared to be working while on the move. They reflected on the nature of "rush hour", the coping strategies people use during this time, and the artistic strategies they could use to capture their observations. During the exhibition installation period, they engaged in a similar action and took detailed notes about the conversations they initiated. The output of their creative research – maps, drawings, and photos from each city paired with an audio account of their encounters in Aberdeen – offered a reflection on the personal and social realities of each city overlaid to remark on similarities intersecting across time and space.

Workplaces at Night was a two-part project that combined investigative research methodologies and candid critical dialogue to eventually form six digital photographic prints and a two-channel video installation. The first part of the project involved the artists visiting various types of workplaces (a hair salon, toy factory, and design studio, among others) to search for residual evidence of humanity after business hours. The artists took photographs and video recordings, but also documented their own activity at these sites. After studying the collected material, the artists engaged in online video chat to discuss what they had discovered, how it had affected their evolving understanding of work, and the way people appear to present their lives and accomplishments in a space that is not genuinely their own.

ABIGAIL SCHONEBOOM, *PROJECT SKIVE*, 2005-2008, MULTIMEDIA INSTALLATION.

English-born/New York-based Abigail Schoneboom's *Project Skive* offered a playful take on workplace dynamics and personal time by exploring what she has referred to as "the creative time-wasting efforts of six English white-collar workers". Skiving is English slang for engaging in non-work activity while on-the-job and derives from the French word *esquiver*, which means "to slink away." Reflecting on the reluctant tolerance of this practice by supervisors, Schoneboom – who has a background in engineering, economics, and sociology – wondered why we spend so much time at work when there isn't always that much to do?

Project Skive began as an online document featuring audio "confessions" from the workers described above. For the exhibition, it grew to invite contributions from visitors to the gallery and online. Tucked away in a dowdy cubicle suggesting the ubiquitous aspects of office culture around the world, gallery visitors were welcome to "waste" as much time as they wished, as if being sneaky and "stealing" time from an imaginary employer. Creating an opportunity to become conscious about a common and under-acknowledged activity, *Project Skive* addressed the notion of "unproductive" time as an appreciation of the fact that time to disengage, procrastinate, and simply *not work* is necessary to retaining intellectual and creative equilibrium.

CATHY BUSBY, *24/7 AT WORK,* 2005, 2008, INSTALLATION-BASED INTERVENTION.

Driven to produce art that responds to the mediation and representation of emotion in consumer culture, Busby's site-specific adaptation of an earlier project, *24/7 at Work*, created a thought-provoking response to the increasing pressure people feel to push themselves, and to the marketplace that makes it "easier" to go harder. Her visual and textual analysis involved the juxtaposition of books about contemporary human resources management and marketing strategies, a range of personal deodorant products, and vinyl lettering declaring the latest management-speak buzz-words in two display cases positioned in the Georgina Scott Sutherland Library at Robert Gordon University, which serves the Faculties of Management and Design.

As Busby points out, if products are a measure of consumer preoccupations, then the pressure to be increasingly available and "on" is clear. Marketers' expropriation of language used by feminist and other social justice movements to speak against oppression is disquieting. For example, the word "empowerment" modified on a toothpaste box to "empowermint," a mint-flavoured toothpaste. However, as Busby points out, workplace management already took a turn at mutating the word when declaring the new worker "empowered" without a union.

Viewed together, the products and books offered a representation of consumers' desire to buy back a little time, strength, and endurance, as well as their search for security and protection. Placing this installation off-site welcomed unsuspecting audiences to consider the issue without the exhibition context and through the course of their daily routine. Busby was approached by students at various times while assembling *24/7 at Work*, and was struck by the number of individuals who immediately read her project as a signal that the library was going to begin selling products, either as a means of subsidizing its primary activity of providing knowledge resources to a future generation of corporate leaders, or as a service to students too busy with their studies to shop for basics. The installation offered opportunities to notice correspondences between work and consumerism.

AMY ALEXANDER, *CYBERSPACELAND*, 2005 – 2008, NEW MEDIA PERFORMANCE-BASED INTERVENTION.

Amy Alexander is an American software and performance artist who created the alter ego VJ Übergeek to respond to various techno-social phenomena. First, society's obsession with wireless technology encourages people to work everywhere and all the time. Second, the fact that people constantly appear to be working (even when playing) by virtue of the fact that the tools of work have become the tools of leisure, making the two activities strangely alike. She describes coffeehouse culture as consisting of lattes and laptops and club performances looking clerical, with laptops replacing guitars, drums, and other "thrashables".

Her audio/visual performance, *CyberSpaceLand*, had previously been performed in night clubs and gallery venues in North America and Europe but for *No Time to Lose*, Alexander decided to deliver this wireless ruckus to people out in the streets. Rather than playing instruments, Alexander generated dance music and visuals by typing on office equipment transported from site to site via a mundane yet unmarked vehicle. Her techno-style eye-candy utilized cheeky internet search queries to reveal the hidden potential for fun and leisure in work tools and modes.

While her performances at three busy locales in Aberdeen didn't inspire a revolution against endless work on the spot, the curious appearance of office furniture, wireless keyboards and mice, and numerous other technological devices adapted to suit Alexander's creative purposes certainly encouraged passersby to stop and enquire about her intentions. Being in "worker drone mode," Alexander was unable to reply, but Peacock Visual Arts employees were on hand to engage in friendly yet serious chat about the nature of work without boundaries and the need for balance to relax, regenerate, socialize, or maybe even just dance.

TOBARON WAXMAN, *BLOCK OF ICE +1/60*, 1999, 2008, NEW MEDIA INSTALLATION AND PERFORMANCE.

Tobaron Waxman is a Canadian interdisciplinary time-based artist, specializing in performance and digital media. First presented in 1999, *Block of Ice* explored his experience with circadian rhythm disorder dyssomnia – a sleep disorder that affects the timing of sleep – to reveal the semi-permeable boundaries between social and personal experiences of health in relation to the social construct of schedule, particularly the notion of daylight hours as the time during which respectable work occurs.

Block of Ice +1/60, a multimedia performance installation in the tradition of tableau vivant, was developed specifically for *No Time to Lose*. The work used the artist's own brainwaves, generated while he slept in the gallery, to control a Max/MSP software patch [developed in partnership with Zachary Seldess] that dynamically located online images pertaining to water and labour. While sleeping throughout the day in a hammock-like sculpture suspended from the ceiling, the artist was monitored by a sensor that collected data generated by the alpha and theta waves emitted by his brain. Processing this data in Max/MSP, the computer program collaged the found online imagery and projected them onto a block of ice. The ice, also suspended from the ceiling, melted through a filtration system and into bottles. Upon waking, Waxman designed a unique label for each bottle featuring the imagery projected earlier. The artist, in effect, worked to create images while asleep, and continued his work upon waking at night. *Block of Ice +1/60* was a performative response to a society that consistently devalues the essentially restorative and creative benefits of sleep for a well functioning mind and body. It furthermore gestured in honour of labourers and shift workers.

PROGRAM OF EVENTS

EXHIBITION PROGRAM

- 13 June – 19 July at Peacock Visual Arts:
  Anja Hertenberger & Anja Steidinger, Saki Satom,
  and Abigail Schoneboom

- 22 – 26 July at Peacock Visual Arts:
  Tobaron Waxman

- 13 June – 26 July at the Georgina Scott
  Sutherland Library, The Robert Gordon
  University: Cathy Busby

EVENTS PROGRAM

- 13 June, 12:30 – 1:30 p.m.
  Discussion at Peacock Visual Arts, with curator
  Milena Placentile and artists Cathy Busby,
  Anja Hertenberger & Anja Steidinger, Saki Satom,
  and Abigail Schoneboom

- 20 June, 5:00 – 9:00 p.m.
  CyberSpaceLand performances
  by Amy Alexander, Locations: The Green
  5:00 p.m., Schoolhill 6:00 p.m.,
  Beach Boulevard 7:00 p.m.

- 8 July, cineclub, Peacock Visual Arts
  7:00 p.m. Short videos

SHORT VIDEOS PRESENTED

Work (1999, 11:00 min) is a digital video shot in
Toronto by ever-lively grrrl filmmaker, Kika Thorne
(Canada), that finds a nonlinear way to reveal the
story of a woman who gets fired from her crummy
office job yet still finds happiness. Each scene is
shot from a slightly different angle and presented
on adjacent screens, so that rather than following
a story from a particular point of view, viewers
experience a series of tableaux. Thorne uses the
open form to multiply the affect of each moment
rather than extend it into narrative.

Coleen Finlayson & Cherie Moses' (Canada) *The
Measure of Success* (1987, 3:15 min) presents the
isolated silhouette of a woman being given a pep
talk apparently intended to help her perform her
job better. However, as the tape progresses, it
becomes clear that the intention of her "superior"
is to demean her performance and manipulate
information to indicate that it is not he who is
displeased with her but the "others". The woman
is always seated and silent and indicates her feeling
through movement alone. This video demonstrates
the struggles many of us endure to conceal our
true selves to please others in unpleasant work-
related situations.

Part two of the trilogy, *The New Freedom Founders,
A Cure for Being Ordinary* (2005, 6:00 min) by Emily
Vey Duke & Cooper Battersby (Canada/USA)
offers an experimental narrative about a young
computer programmer and his reflections
on capitalism and its impact on our collective
perceptions of time. Through this, he shares insight
into how to world of work functions, how we're
trapped in its mechanisms, and eventually, what
we can do to become free.

Leila Sujir's (India/Canada) *The Dreams of the Night
Cleaners* (1995, 46:00 min) offers a journey through
history and memory. A complex weave of drama,
archival footage, and animation in a fable format, it
explores the public mythologies in North American
culture that have had devastating effects on public
policy, public attitudes, and individual lives. Using
storytelling, humour, magic, and history to sweep
away the misconceptions which haunt the lives of
its characters, this video addresses fears of job loss
in an uncertain marketplace, feelings of insecurity
and unstable identity due to their uncertain
economic positions, as well as experiences of
racism and sexism. It illuminates the reality of work
as a means to an end, but not as a reflection of
ourselves, our hopes, and our dreams.

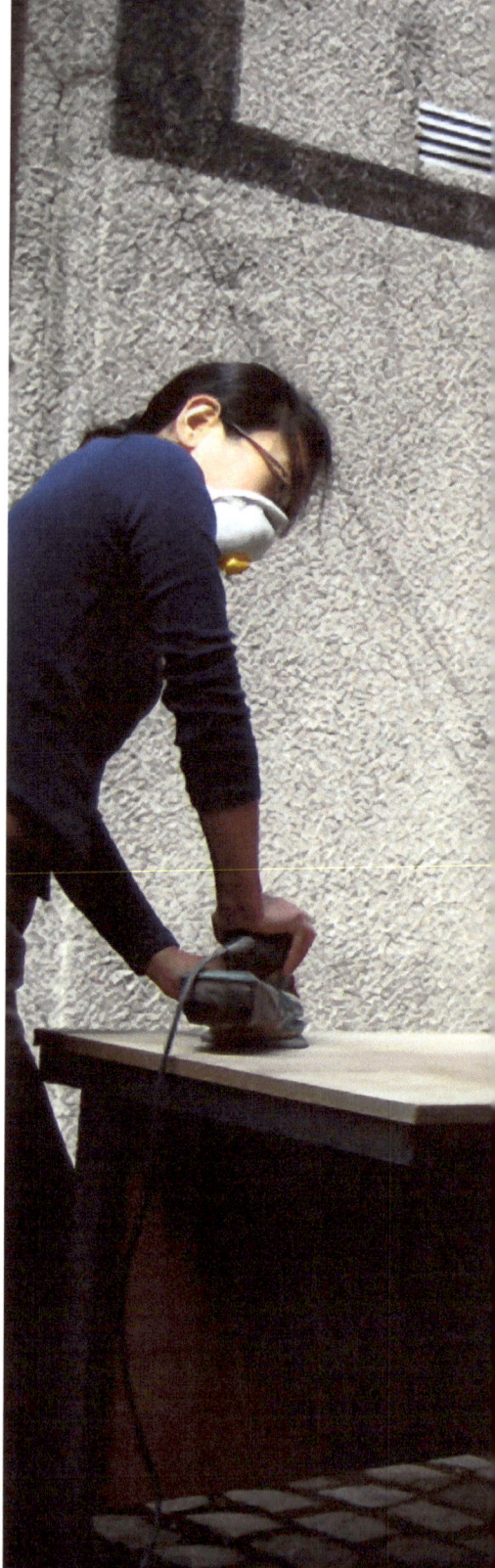

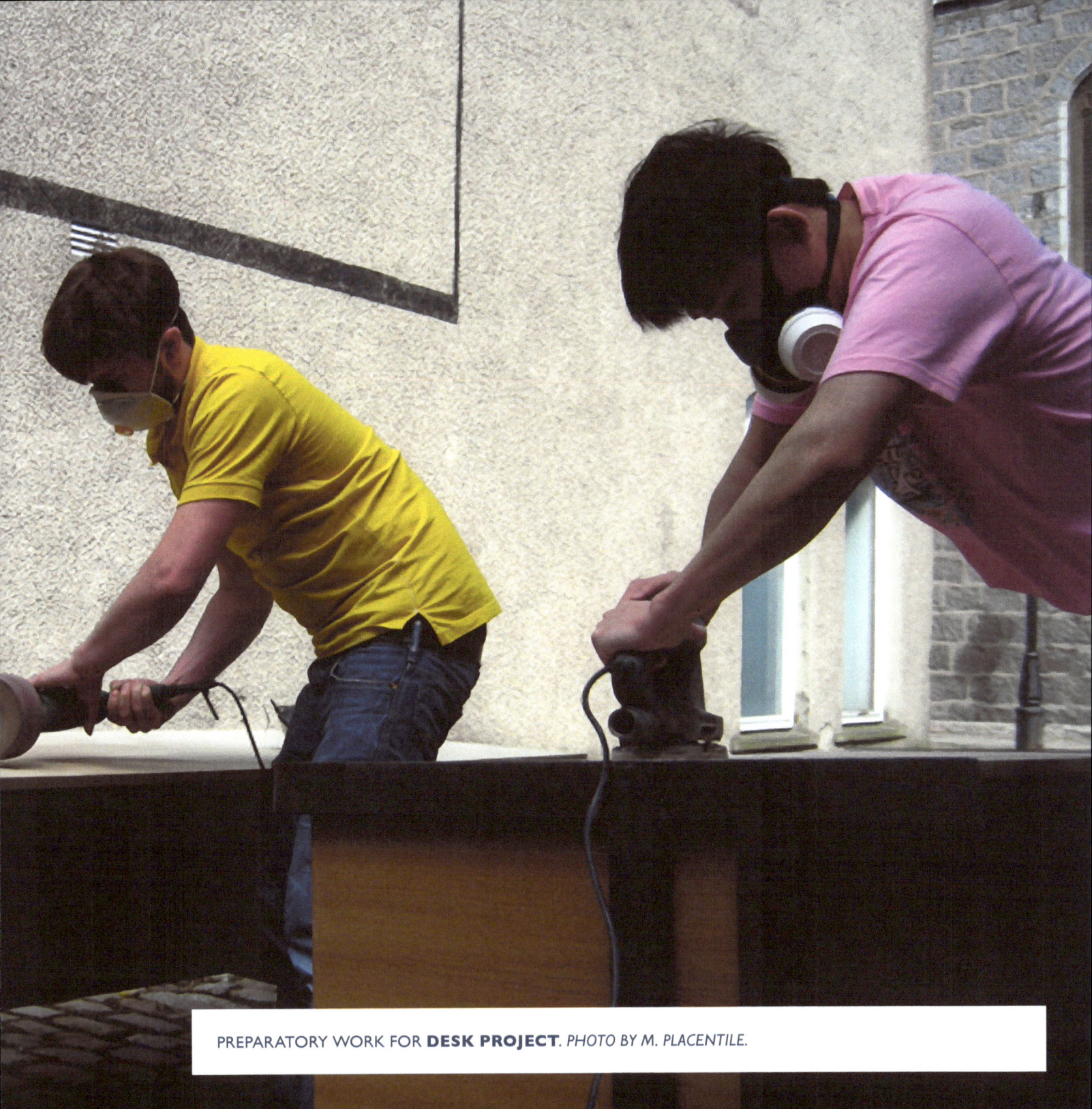

PREPARATORY WORK FOR **DESK PROJECT**. *PHOTO BY M. PLACENTILE.*

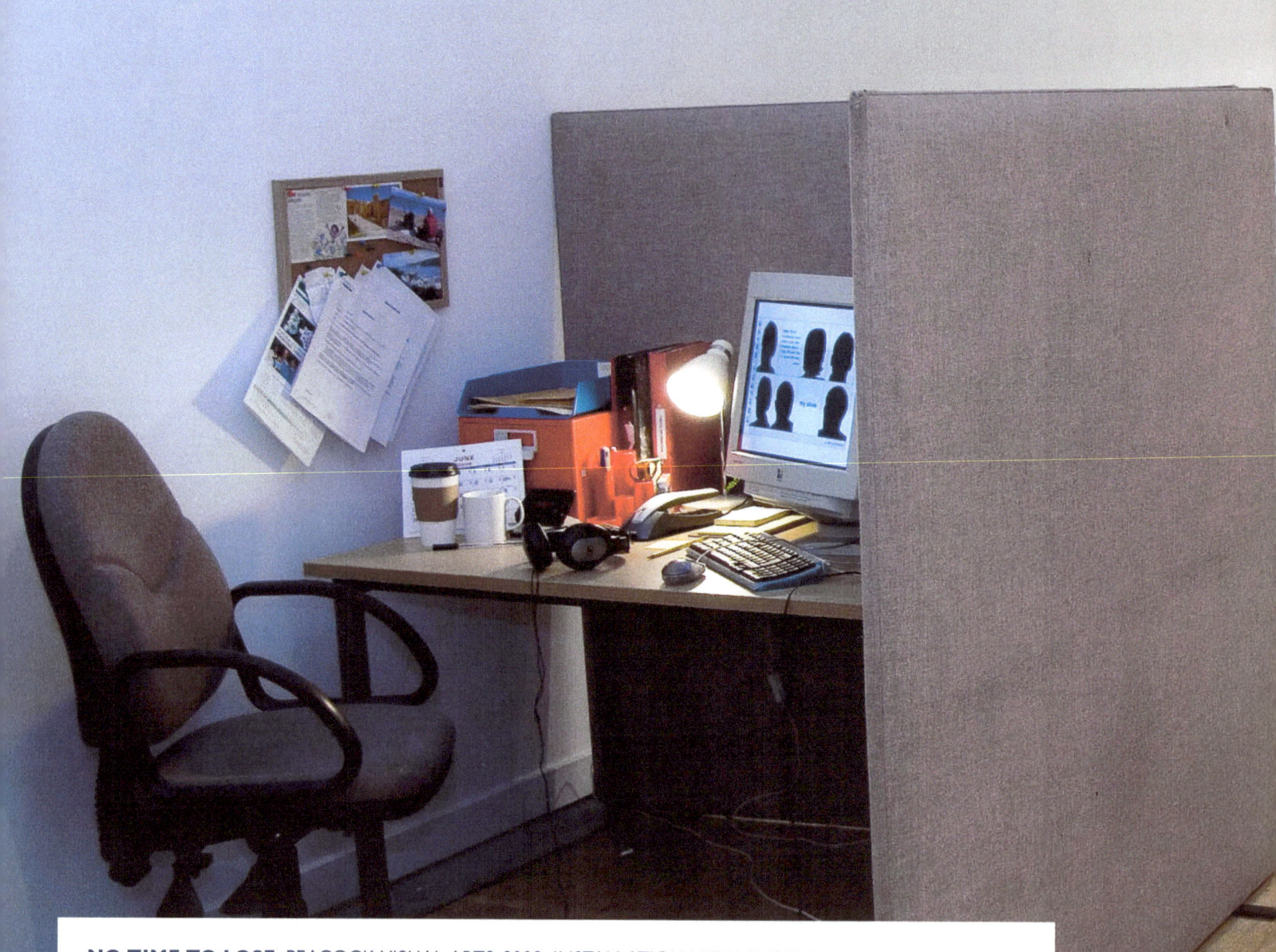

NO TIME TO LOSE, PEACOCK VISUAL ARTS, 2008. INSTALLATION VIEW. *PHOTO BY T. KETTLE.*

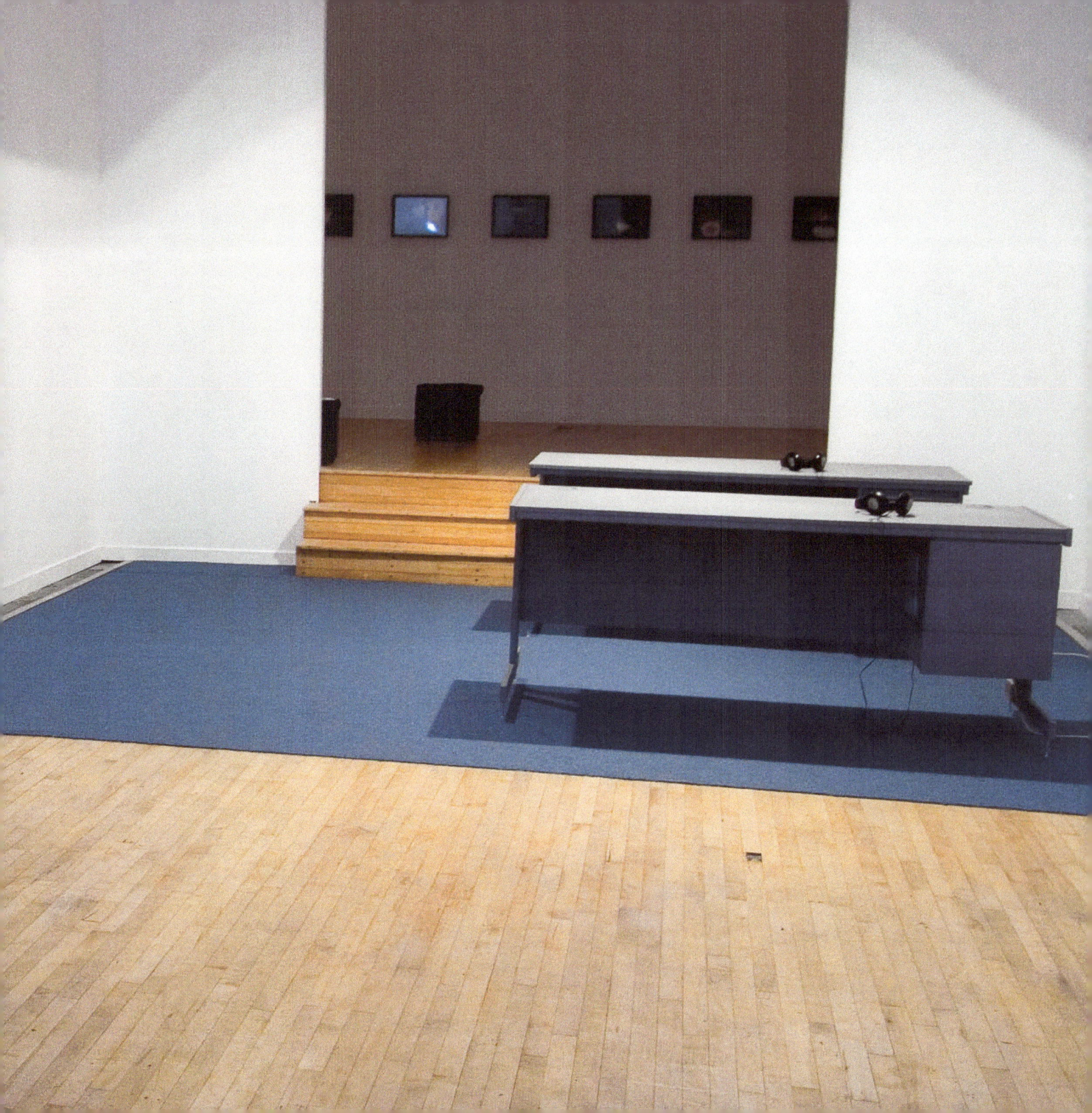

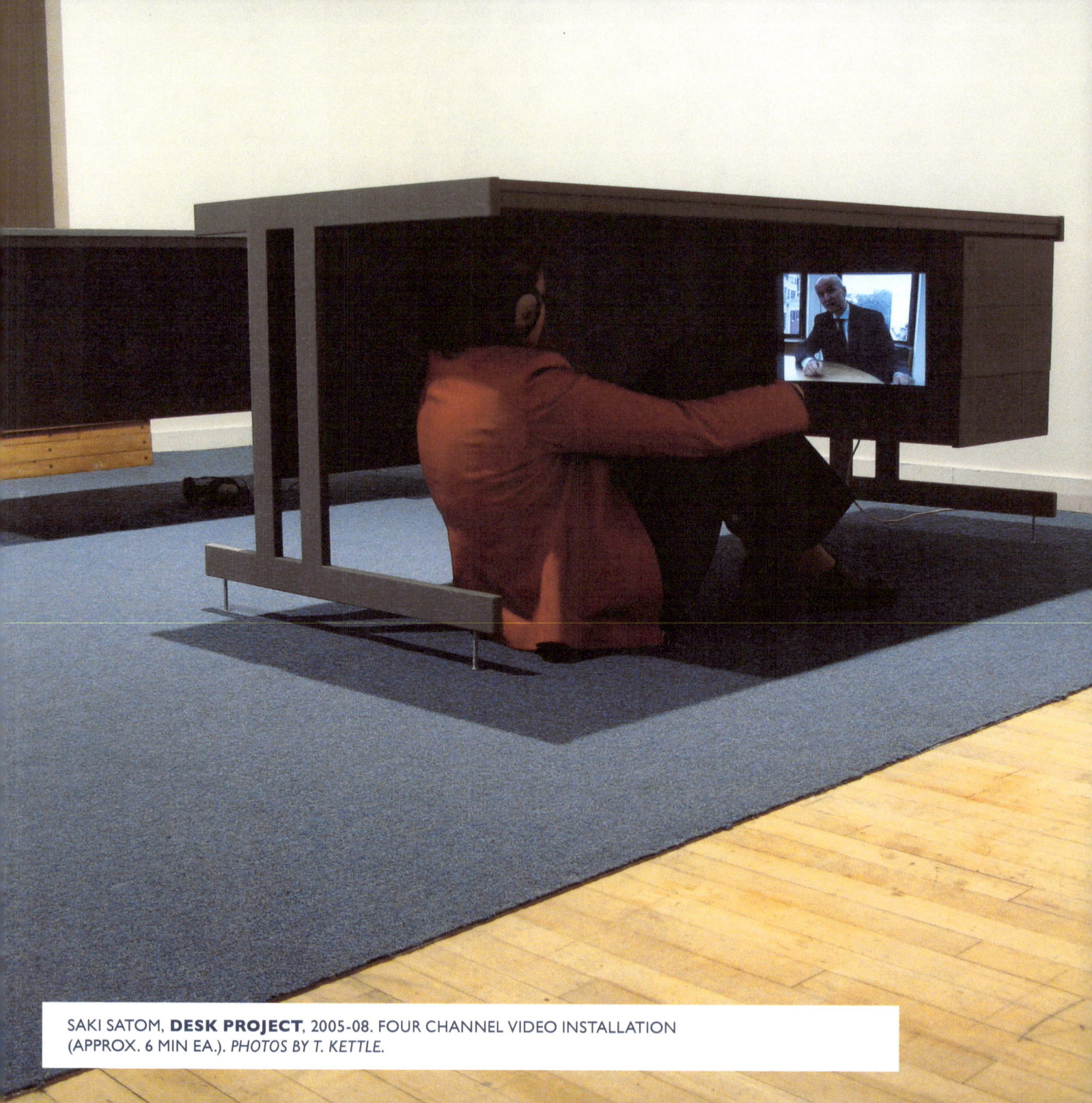

SAKI SATOM, **DESK PROJECT**, 2005-08. FOUR CHANNEL VIDEO INSTALLATION
(APPROX. 6 MIN EA.). *PHOTOS BY T. KETTLE.*

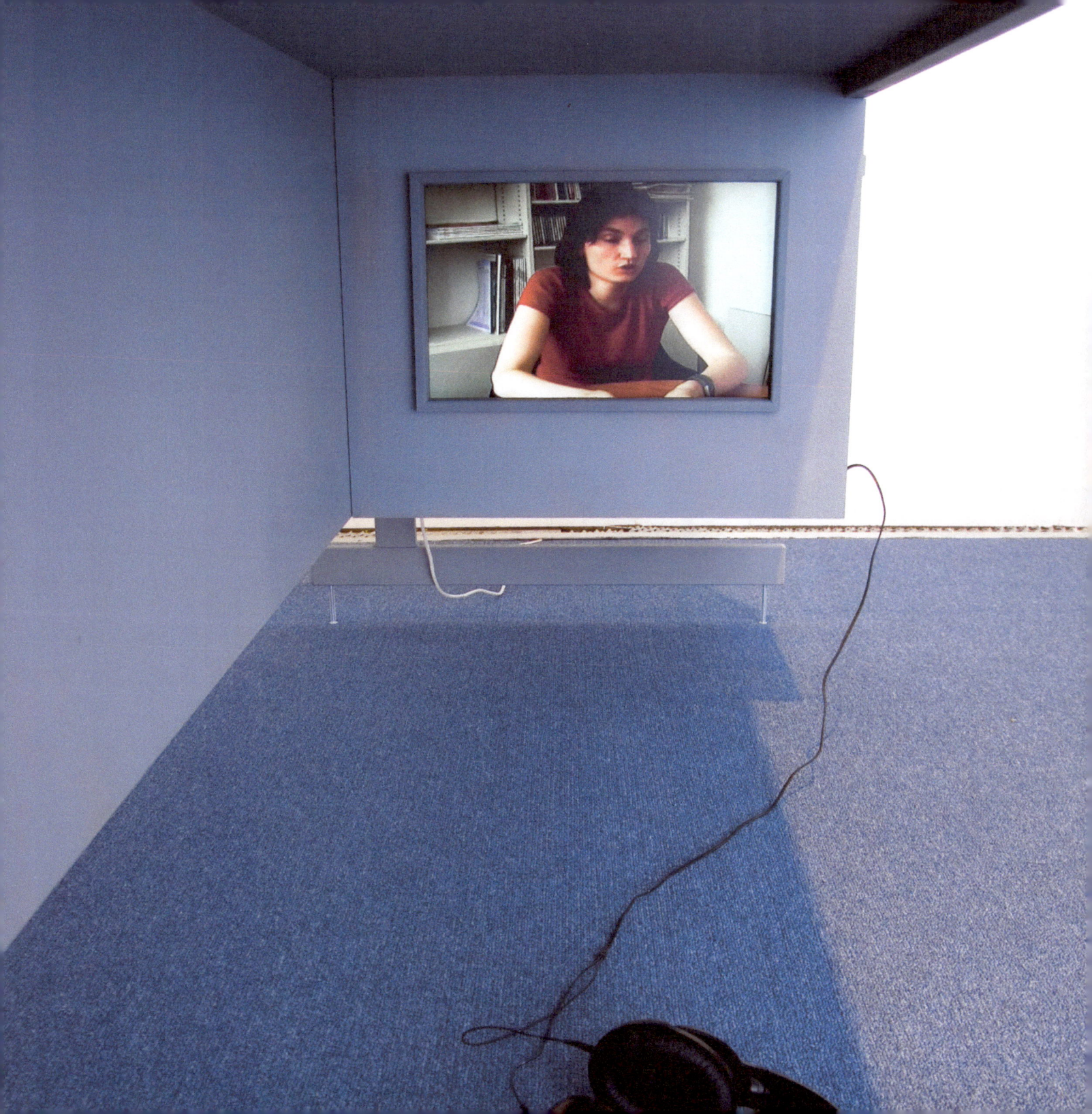

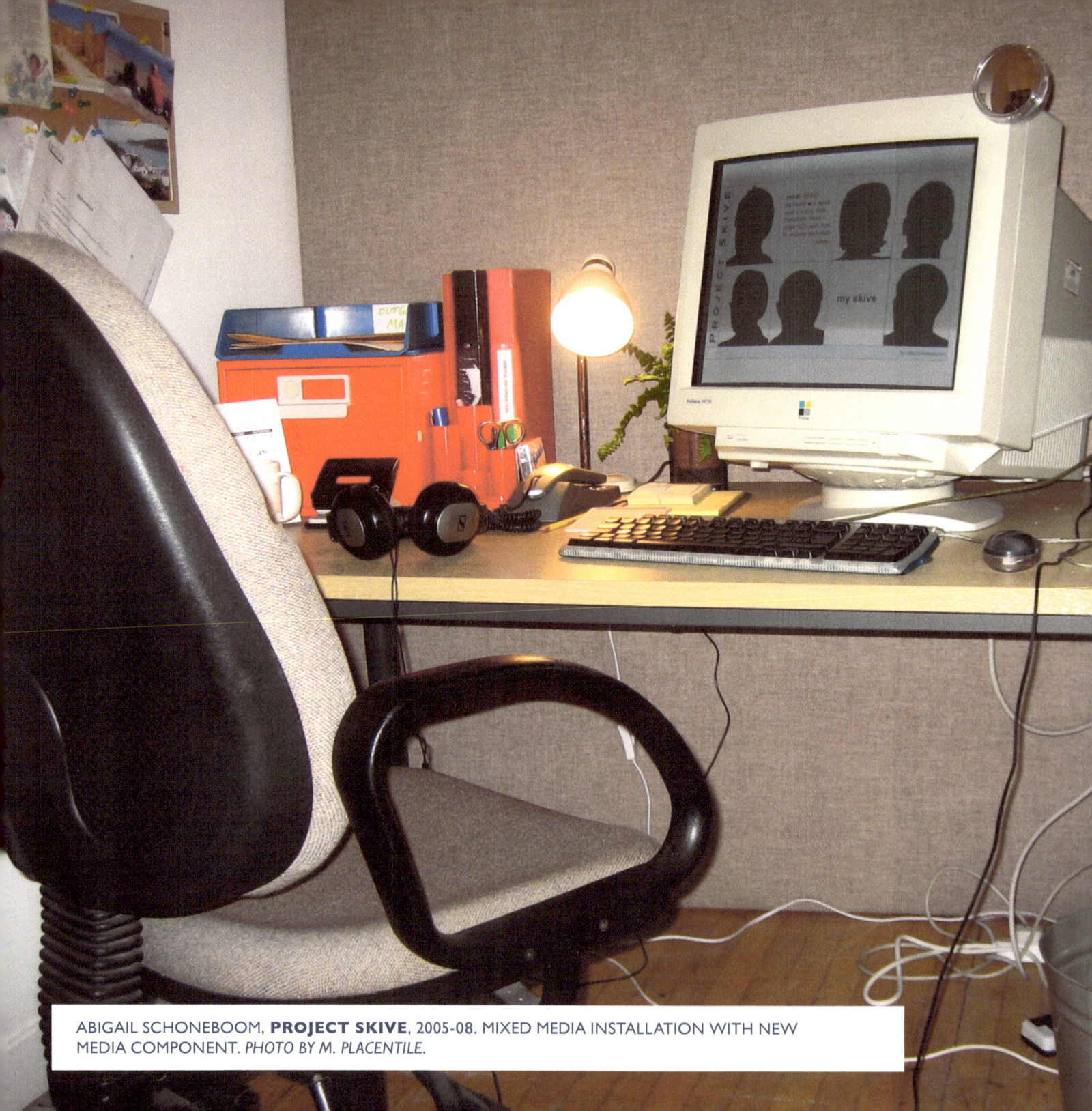

ABIGAIL SCHONEBOOM, **PROJECT SKIVE**, 2005-08. MIXED MEDIA INSTALLATION WITH NEW MEDIA COMPONENT. *PHOTO BY M. PLACENTILE.*

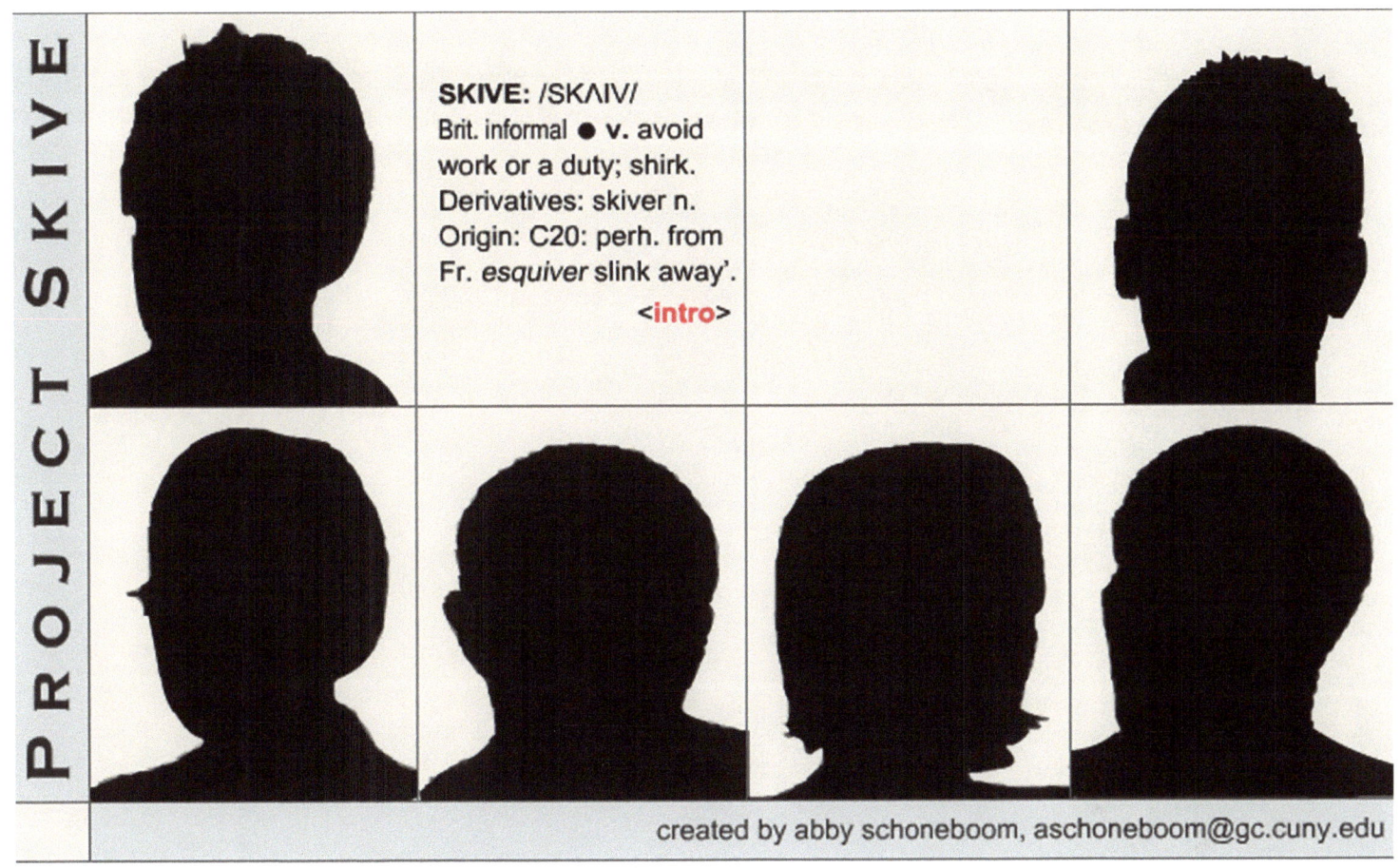

SKIVE: /SKΛIV/
Brit. informal ● v. avoid
work or a duty; shirk.
Derivatives: skiver n.
Origin: C20: perh. from
Fr. *esquiver* slink away'.
<intro>

created by abby schoneboom, aschoneboom@gc.cuny.edu

ABIGAIL SCHONEBOOM, **PROJECT SKIVE**, 2005-08. *SCREEN CAPTURE COURTESY OF THE ARTIST.*

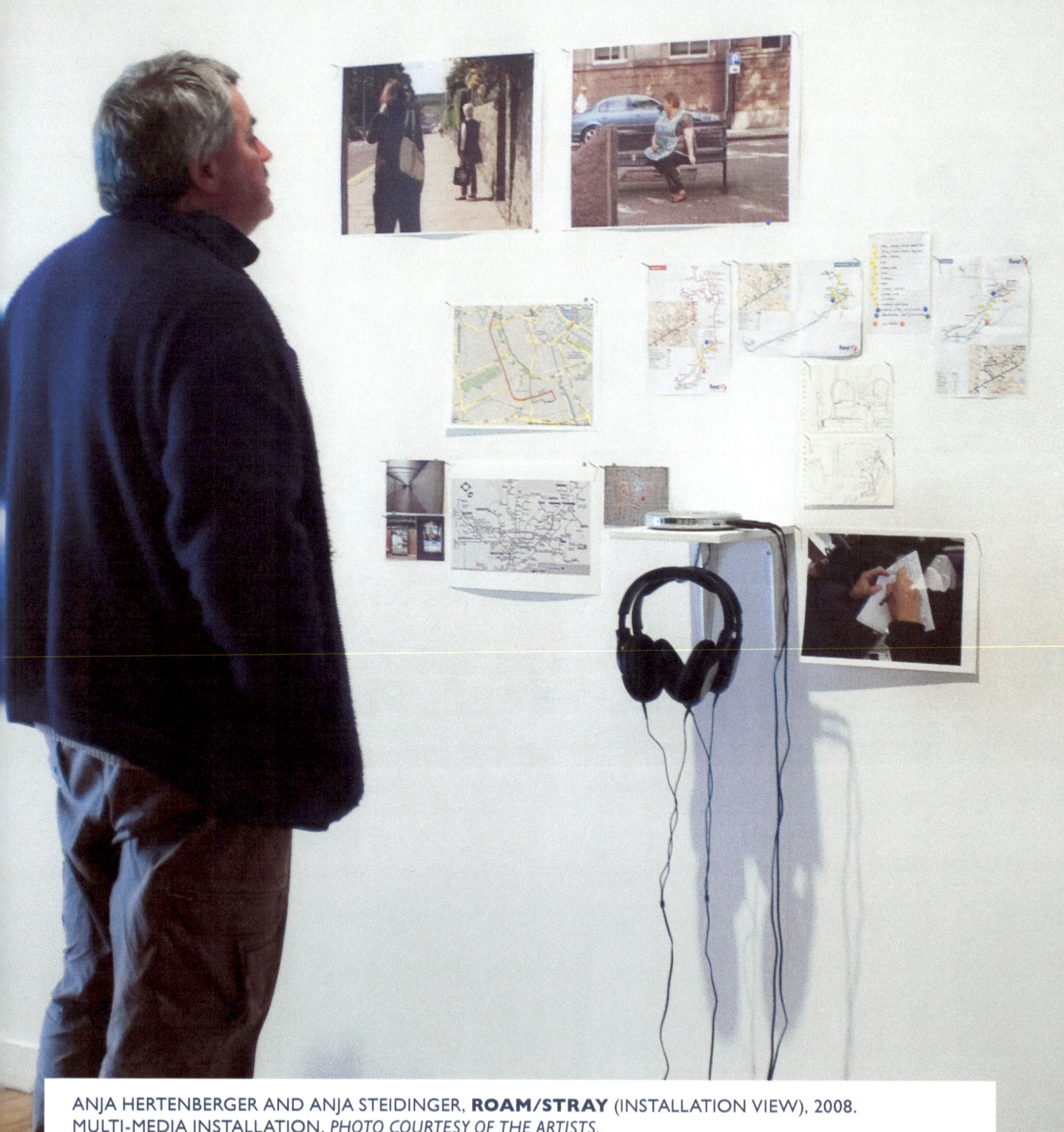

ANJA HERTENBERGER AND ANJA STEIDINGER, **ROAM/STRAY** (INSTALLATION VIEW), 2008.
MULTI-MEDIA INSTALLATION. *PHOTO COURTESY OF THE ARTISTS.*

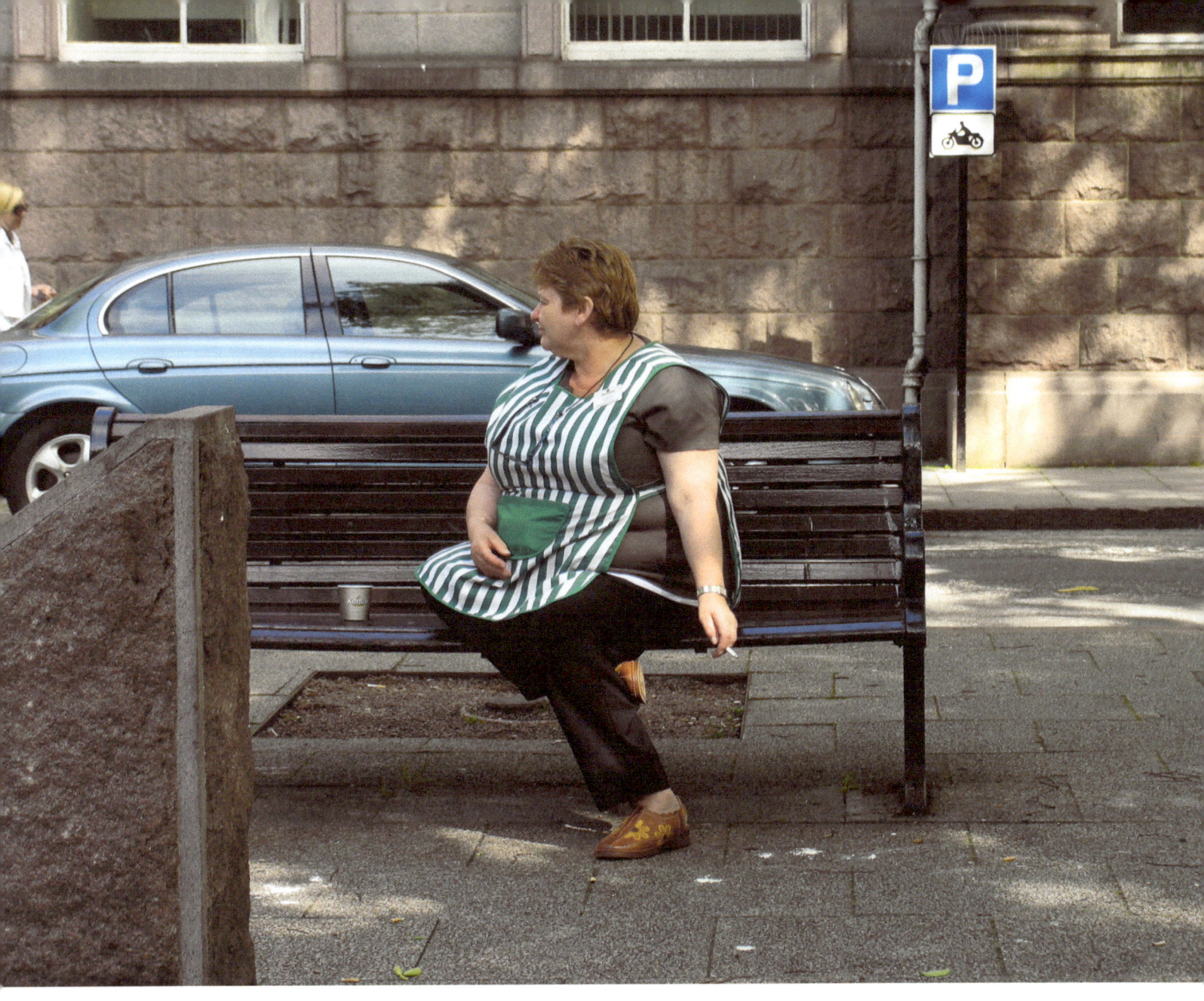

ANJA HERTENBERGER AND ANJA STEIDINGER, **ROAM/STRAY** (DETAIL), 2008. DIGITAL PRINT INCLUDED AS PART OF MULTI-MEDIA INSTALLATION. *PHOTO COURTESY OF THE ARTISTS.*

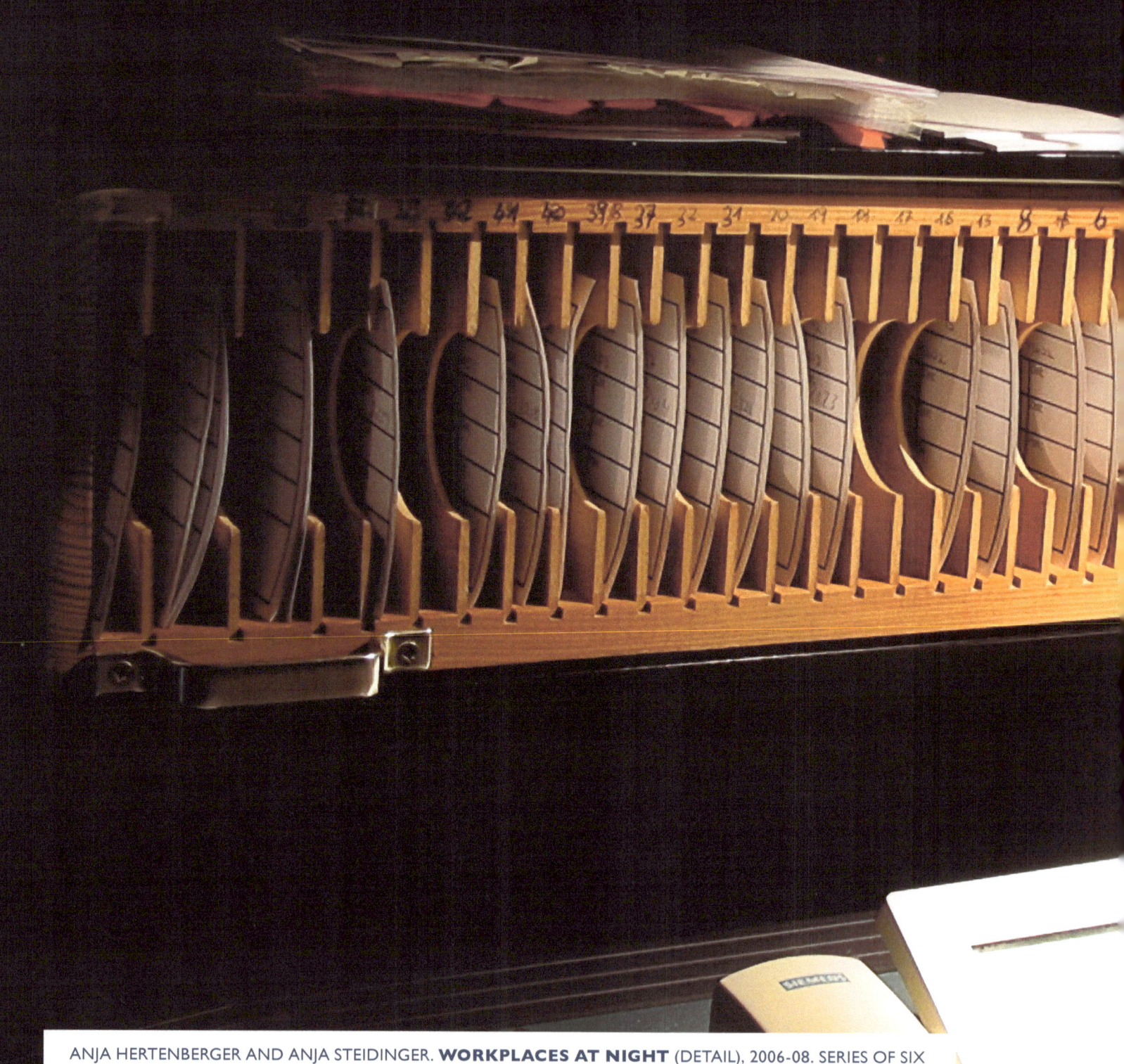

ANJA HERTENBERGER AND ANJA STEIDINGER. **WORKPLACES AT NIGHT** (DETAIL), 2006-08. SERIES OF SIX DIGITAL PRINTS INCLUDED AS PART OF A MULTI-MEDIA INSTALLATION. *PHOTO COURTESY OF THE ARTISTS.*

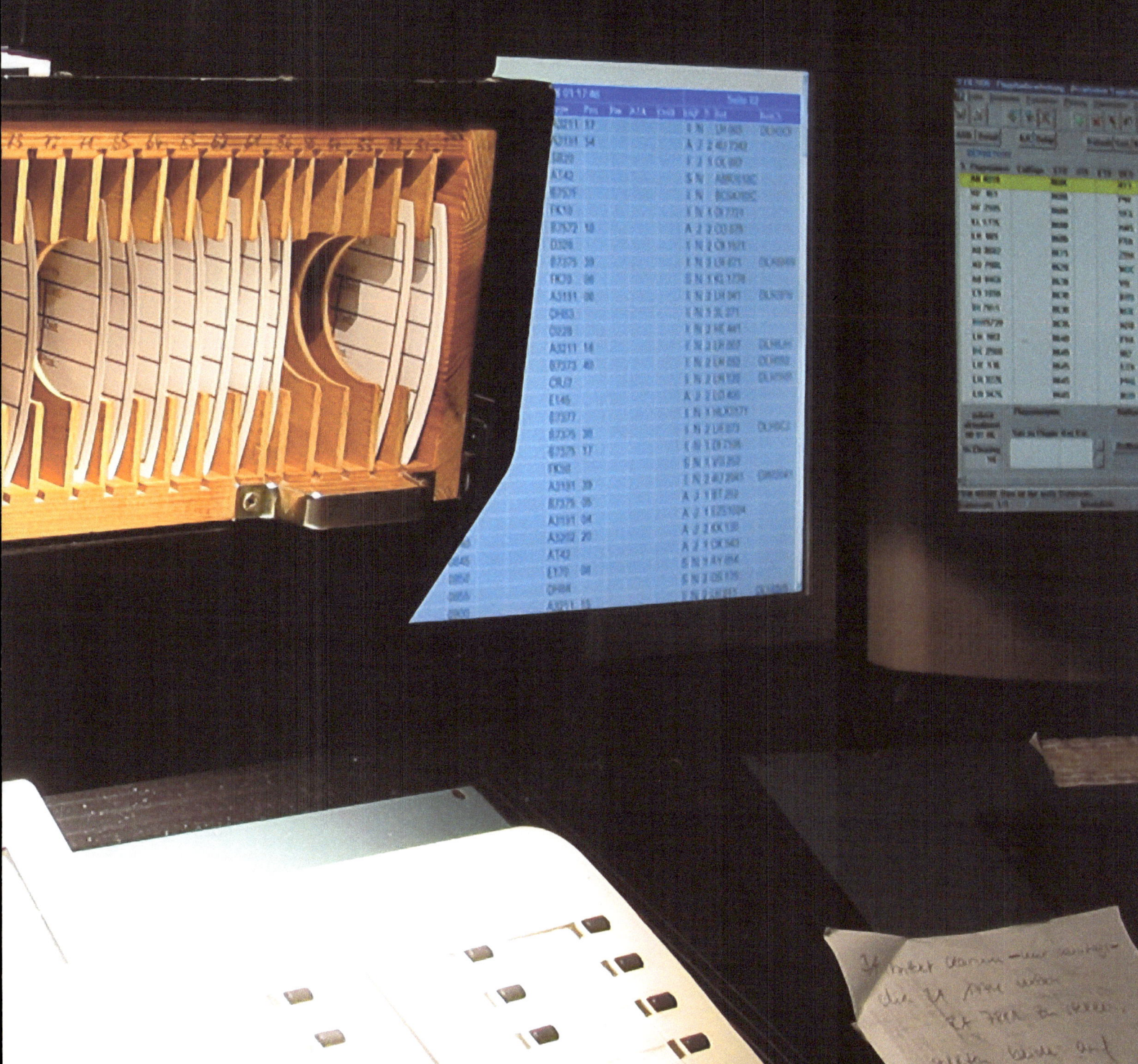

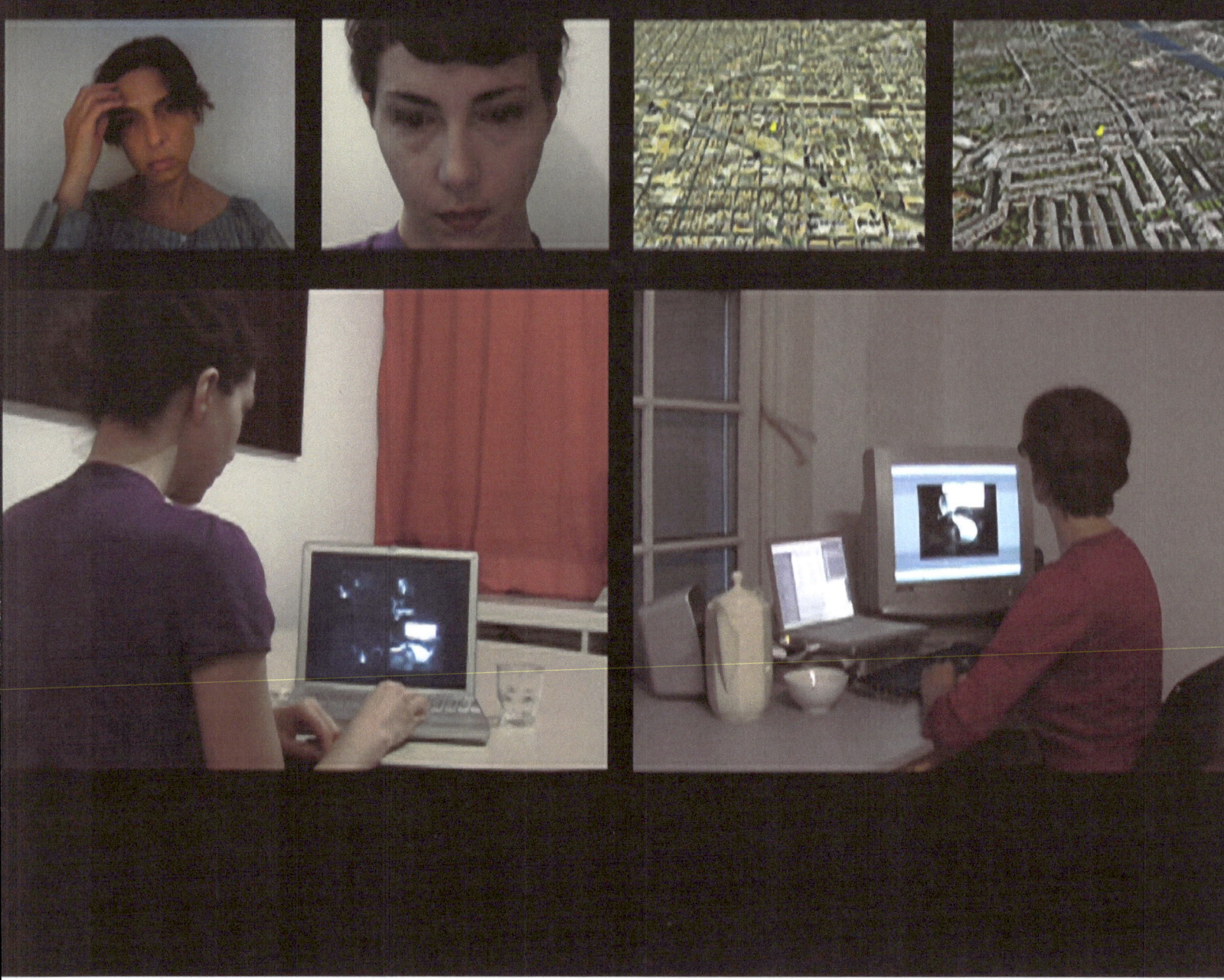

ANJA HERTENBERGER AND ANJA STEIDINGER. **WORKPLACES AT NIGHT** (VIDEO STILLS), 2006-08. TWO CHANNEL VIDEO INCLUDED AS PART OF A MULTI-MEDIA INSTALLATION. *IMAGES COURTESY OF THE ARTISTS.*

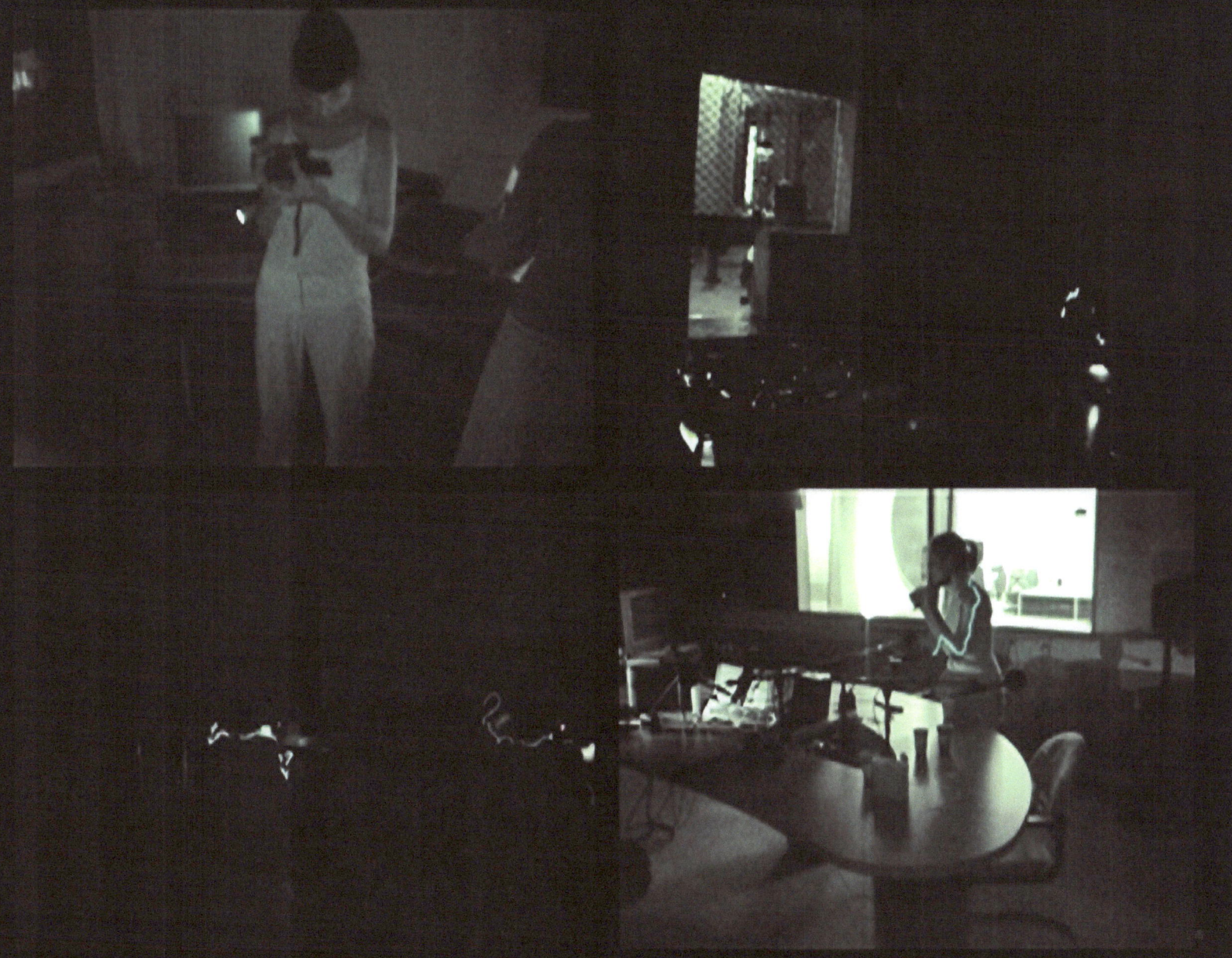

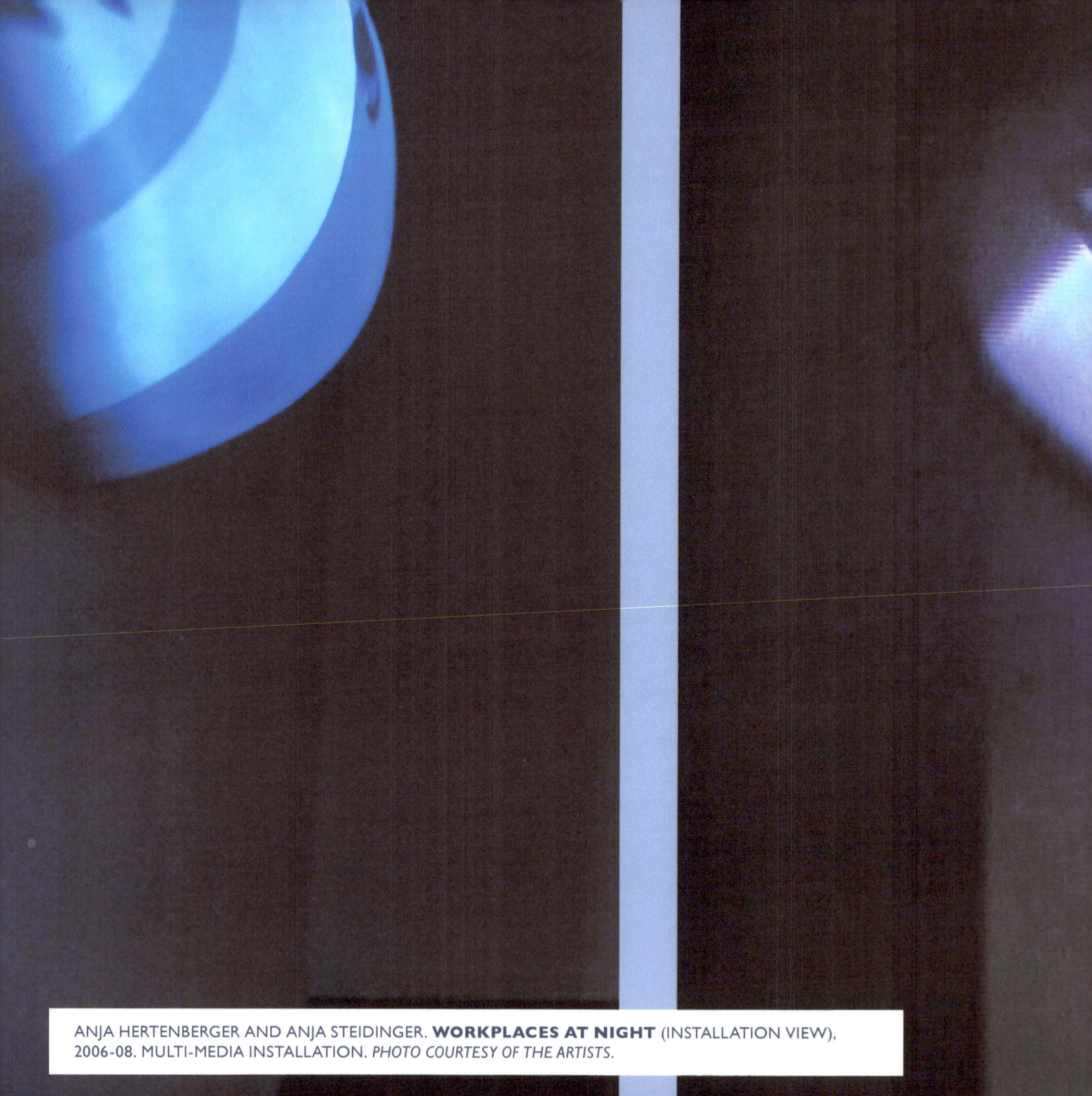

ANJA HERTENBERGER AND ANJA STEIDINGER. **WORKPLACES AT NIGHT** (INSTALLATION VIEW), 2006-08. MULTI-MEDIA INSTALLATION. *PHOTO COURTESY OF THE ARTISTS.*

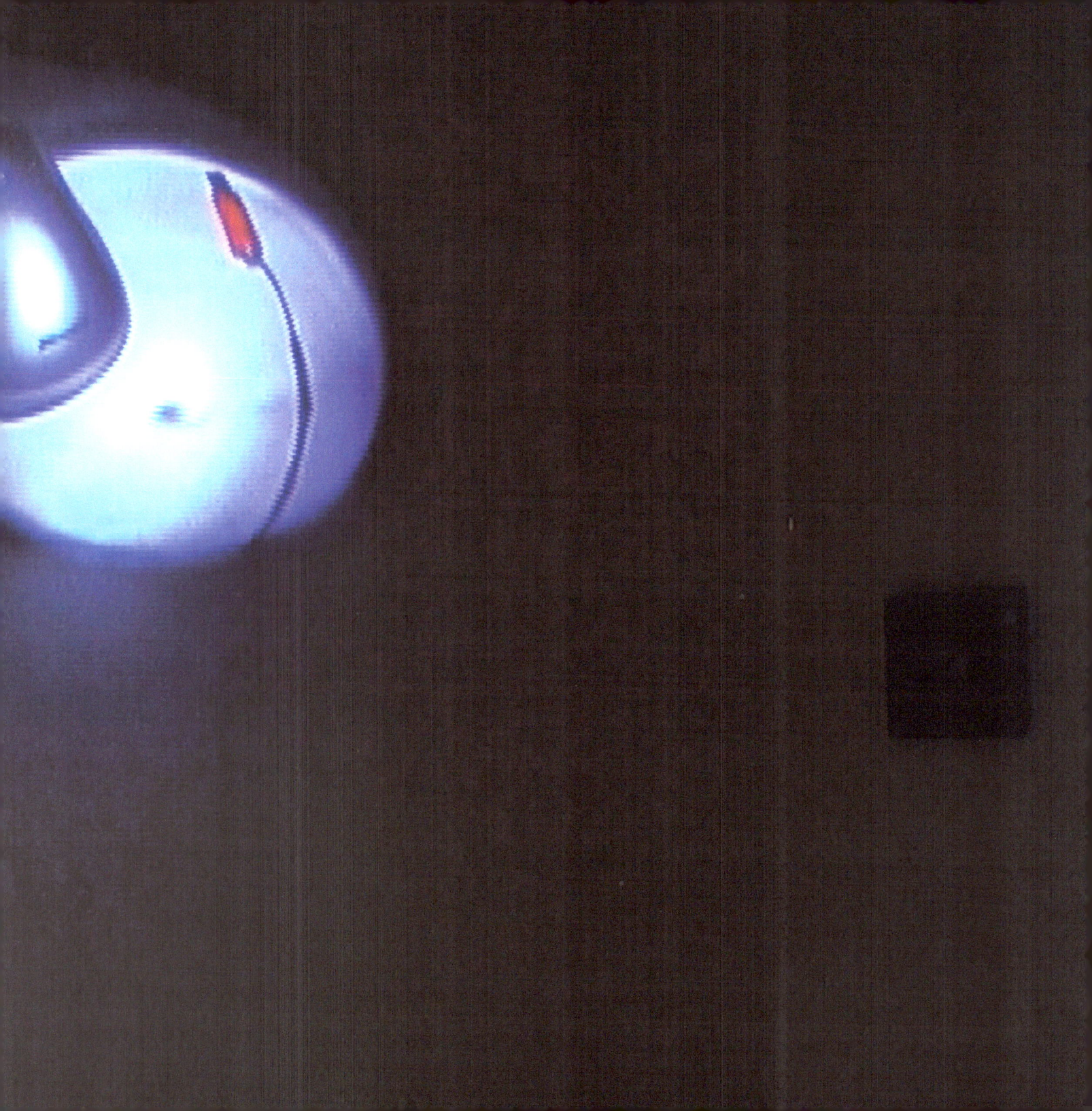

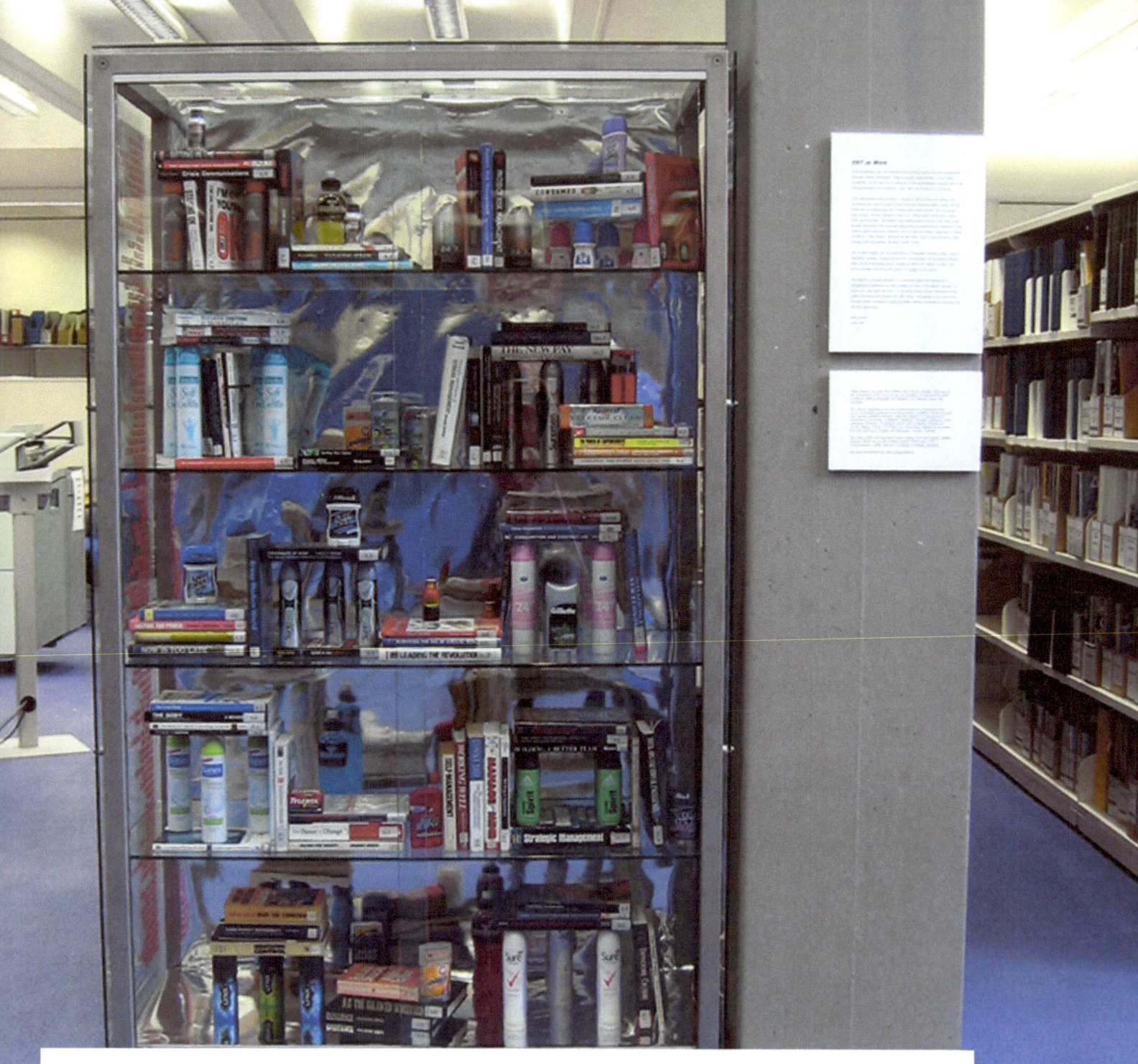

CATHY BUSBY, **24/7 AT WORK**, 2008. FOUND OBJECT INSTALLATION-BASED INTERVENTION, GEORGINA SCOTT SUTHERLAND LIBRARY AT ROBERT GORDON UNIVERSITY, ABERDEEN. *PHOTOS COURTESY OF THE ARTIST.*

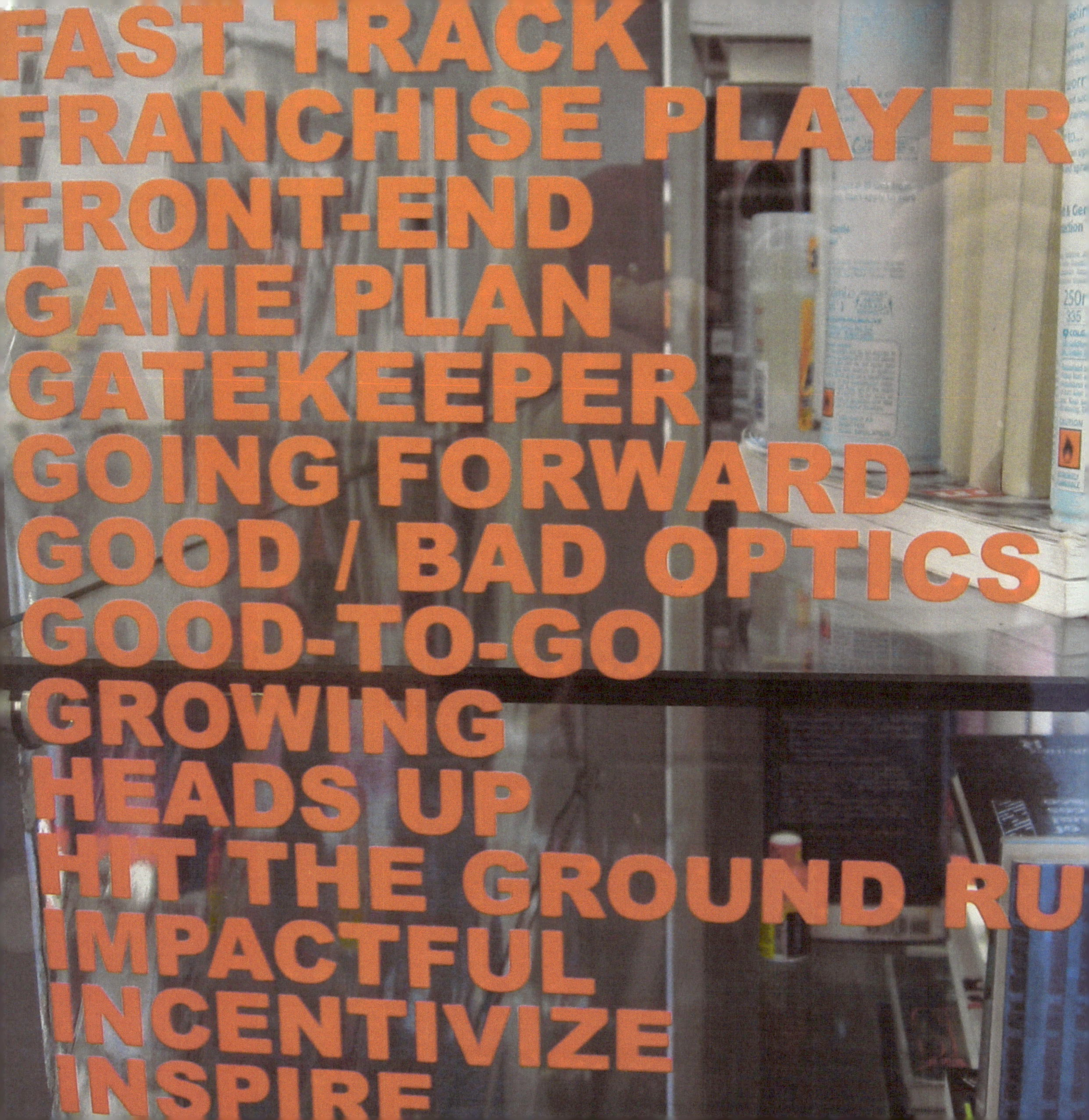

FAST TRACK
FRANCHISE PLAYER
FRONT-END
GAME PLAN
GATEKEEPER
GOING FORWARD
GOOD / BAD OPTICS
GOOD-TO-GO
GROWING
HEADS UP
HIT THE GROUND RU
IMPACTFUL
INCENTIVIZE
INSPIRE

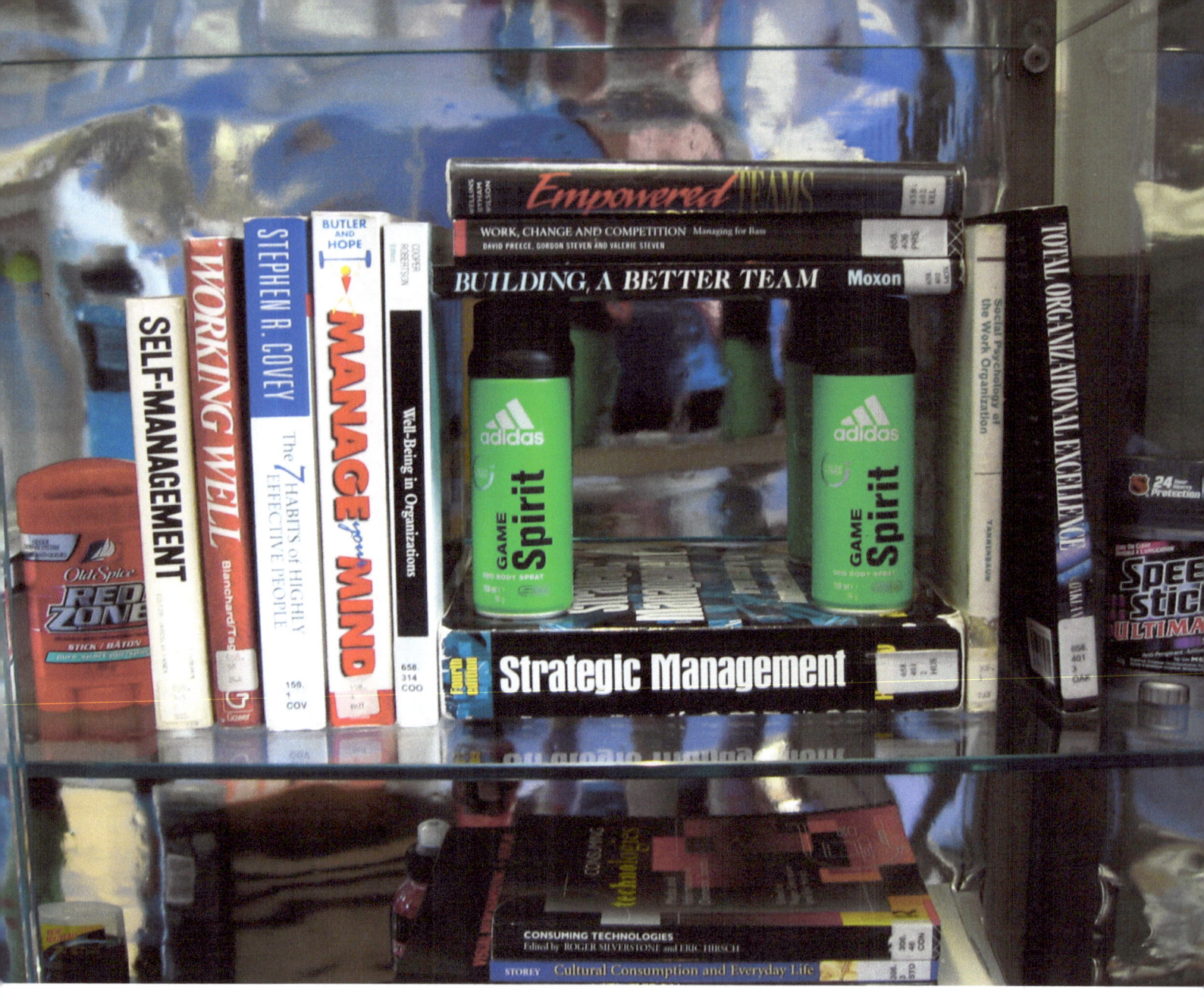

CATHY BUSBY, **24/7 AT WORK**, 2008. FOUND OBJECT INSTALLATION-BASED INTERVENTION, GEORGINA SCOTT SUTHERLAND LIBRARY AT ROBERT GORDON UNIVERSITY, ABERDEEN. *PHOTOS COURTESY OF THE ARTIST.*

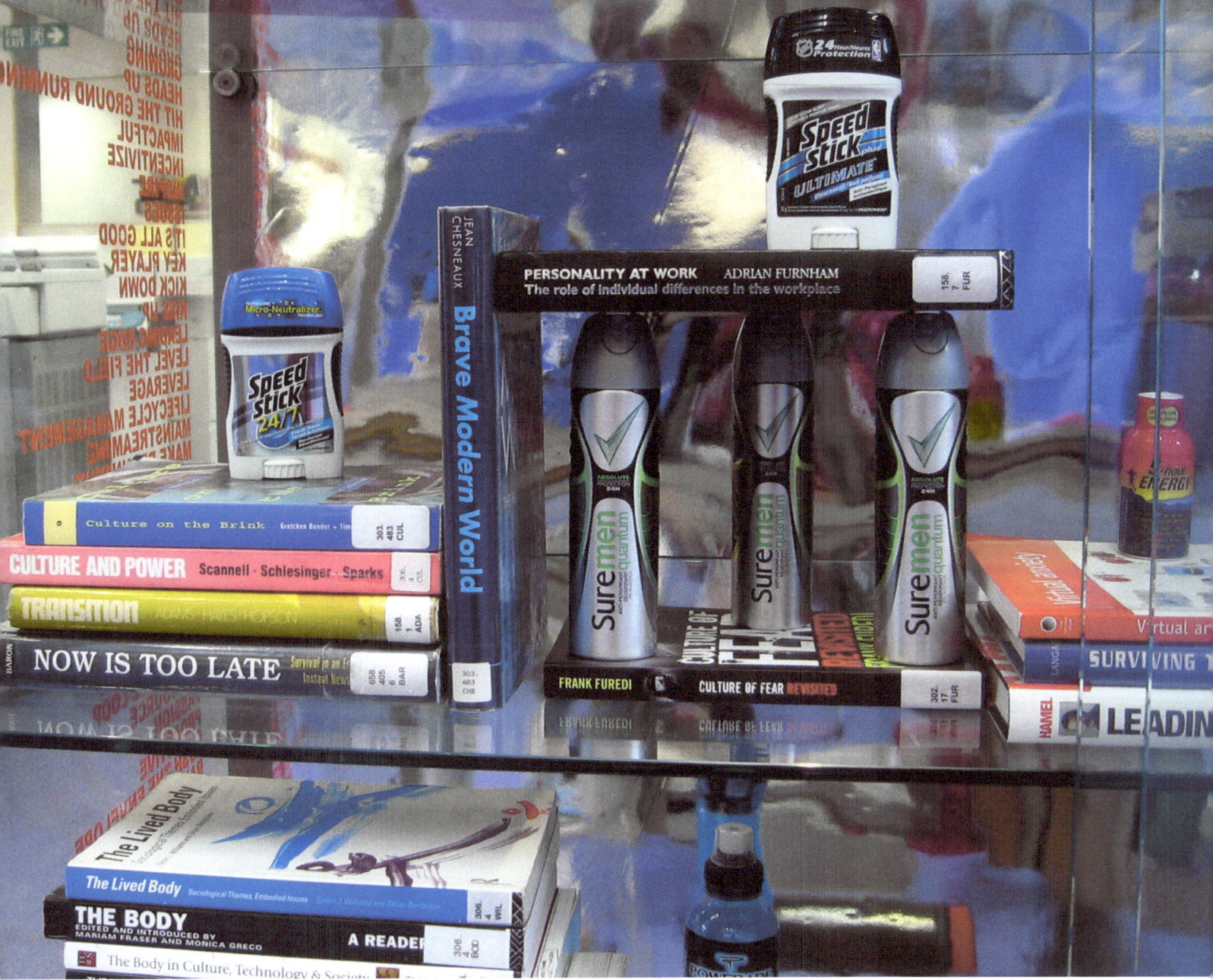

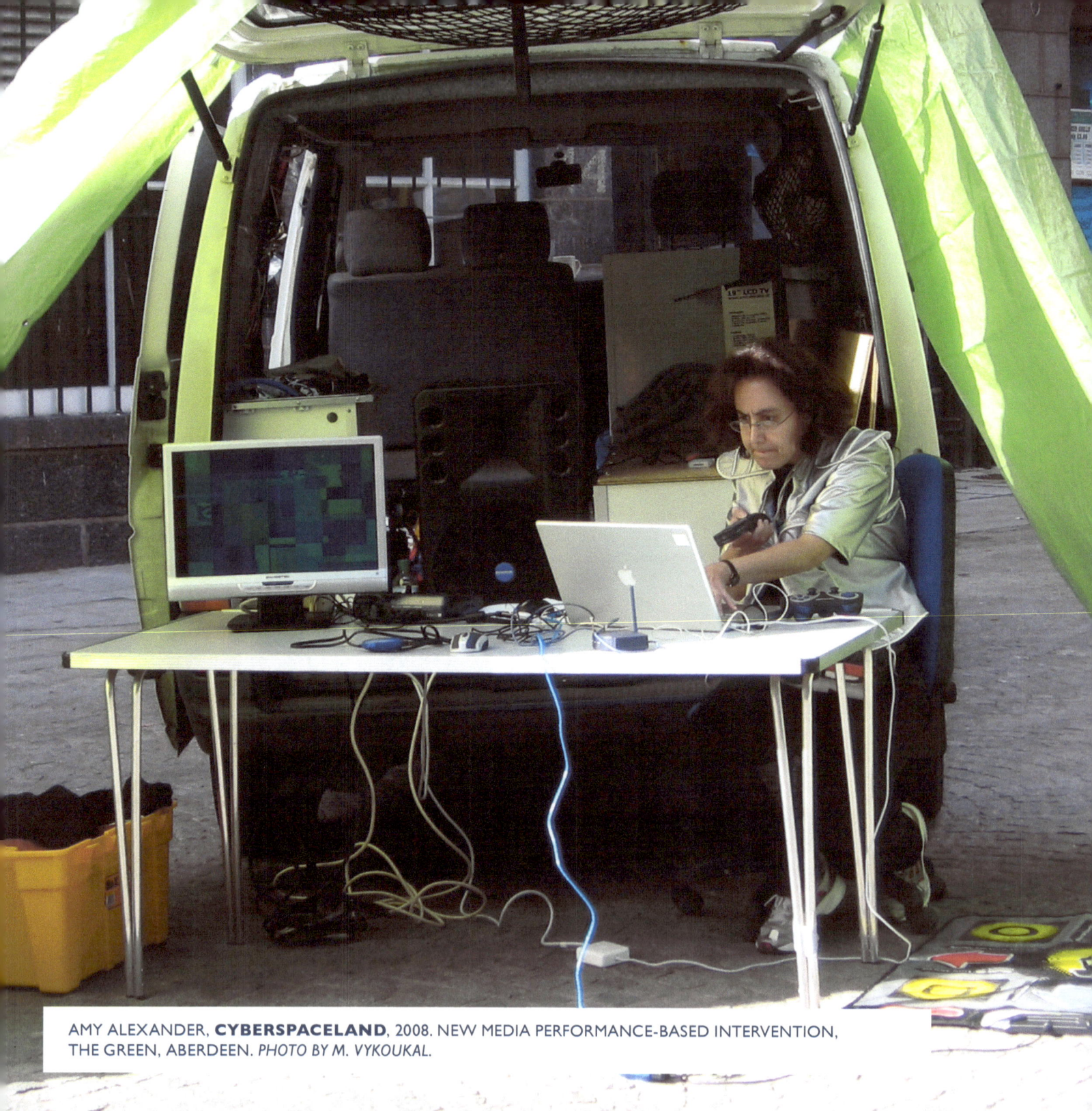

AMY ALEXANDER, **CYBERSPACELAND**, 2008. NEW MEDIA PERFORMANCE-BASED INTERVENTION, THE GREEN, ABERDEEN. *PHOTO BY M. VYKOUKAL.*

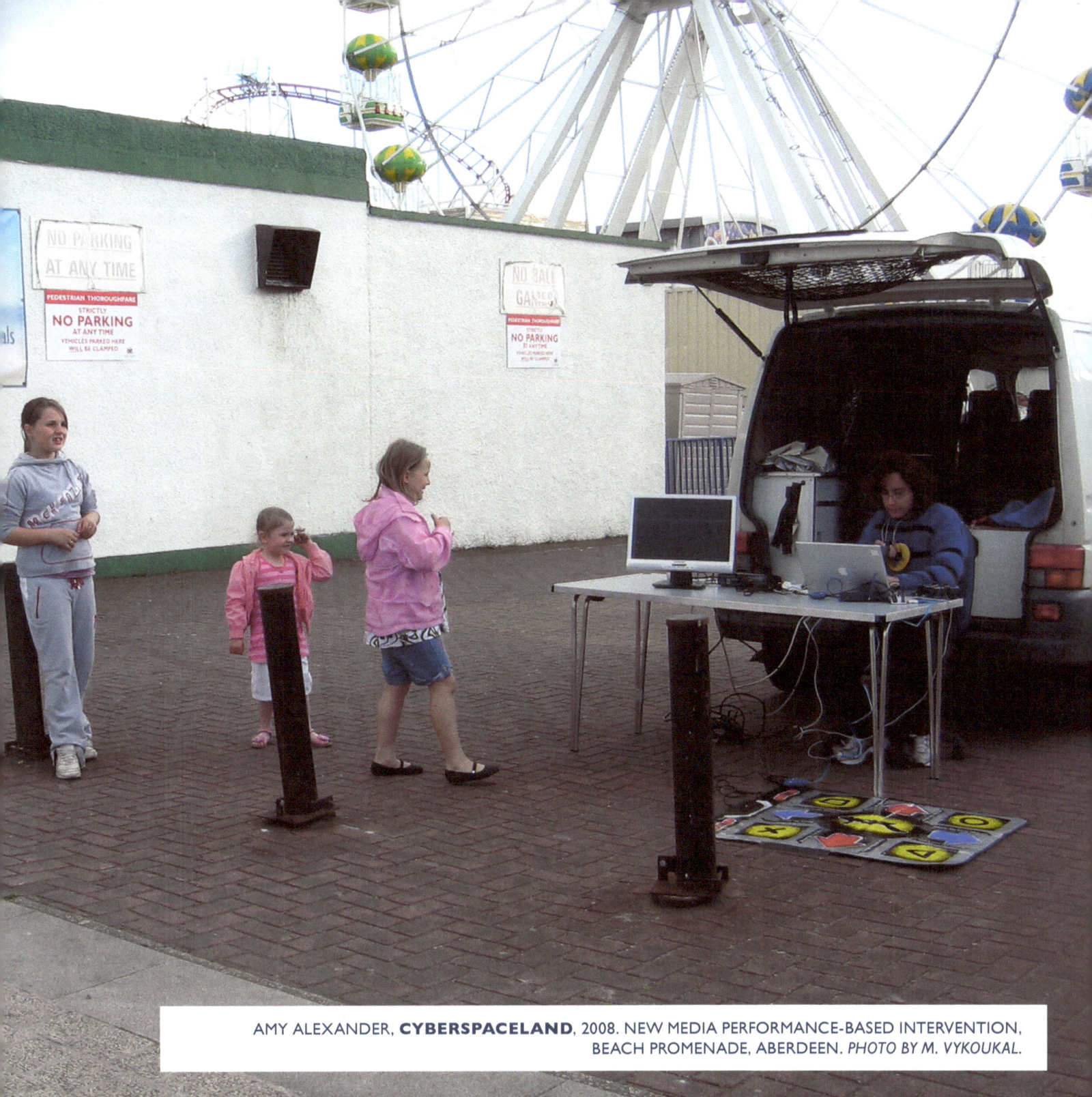

AMY ALEXANDER, **CYBERSPACELAND**, 2008. NEW MEDIA PERFORMANCE-BASED INTERVENTION, BEACH PROMENADE, ABERDEEN. *PHOTO BY M. VYKOUKAL.*

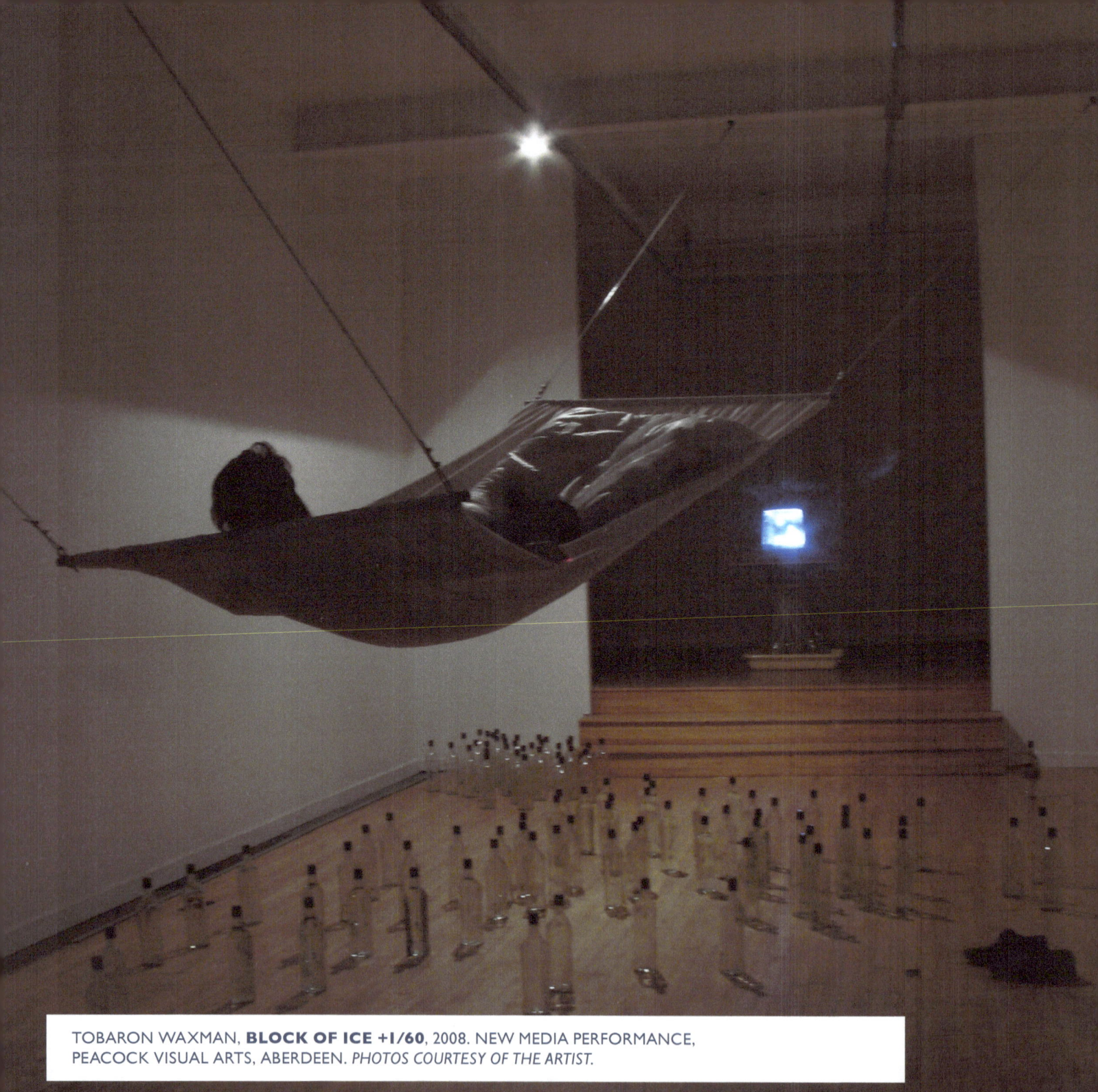

TOBARON WAXMAN, **BLOCK OF ICE +1/60**, 2008. NEW MEDIA PERFORMANCE, PEACOCK VISUAL ARTS, ABERDEEN. *PHOTOS COURTESY OF THE ARTIST.*

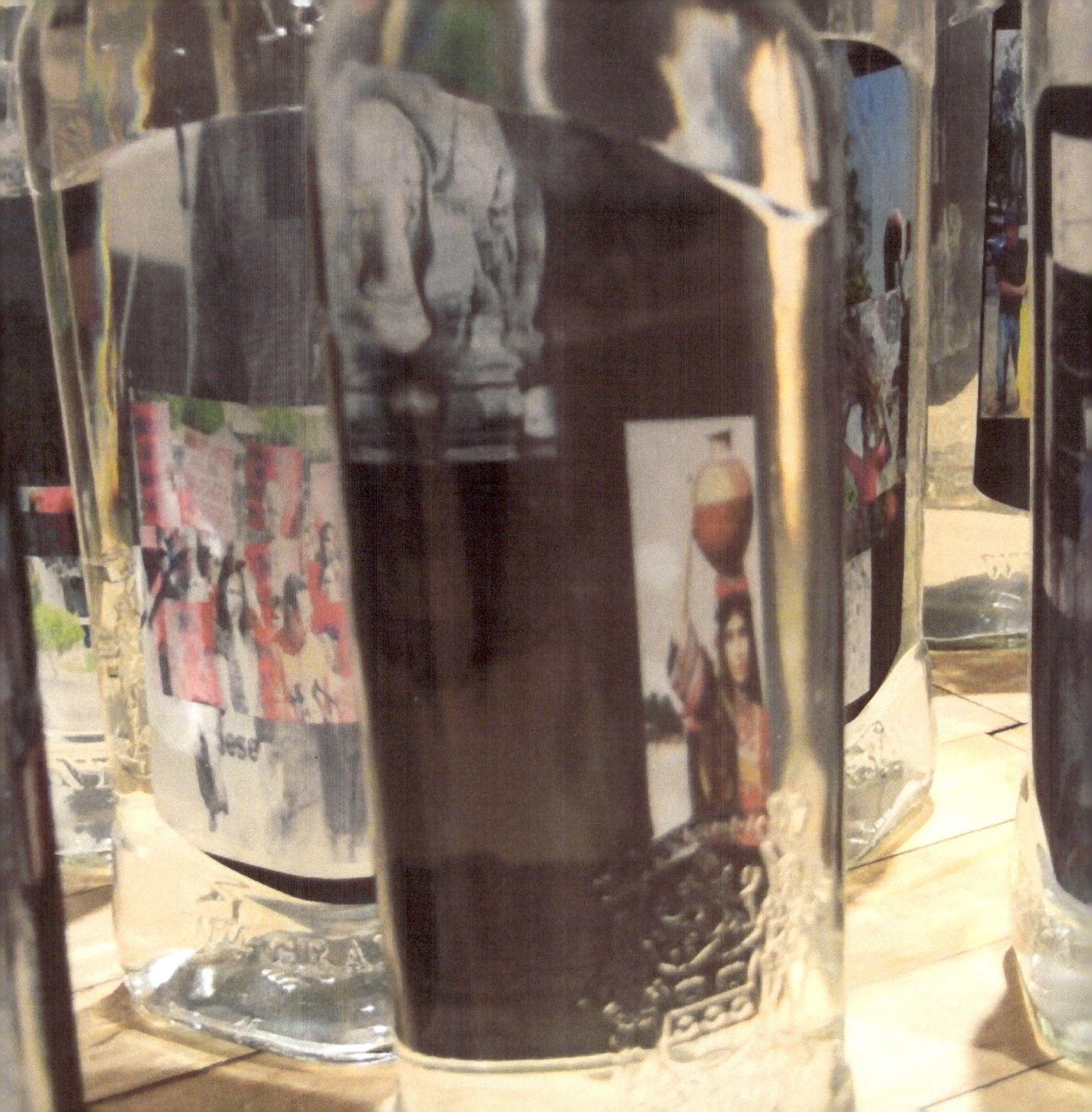

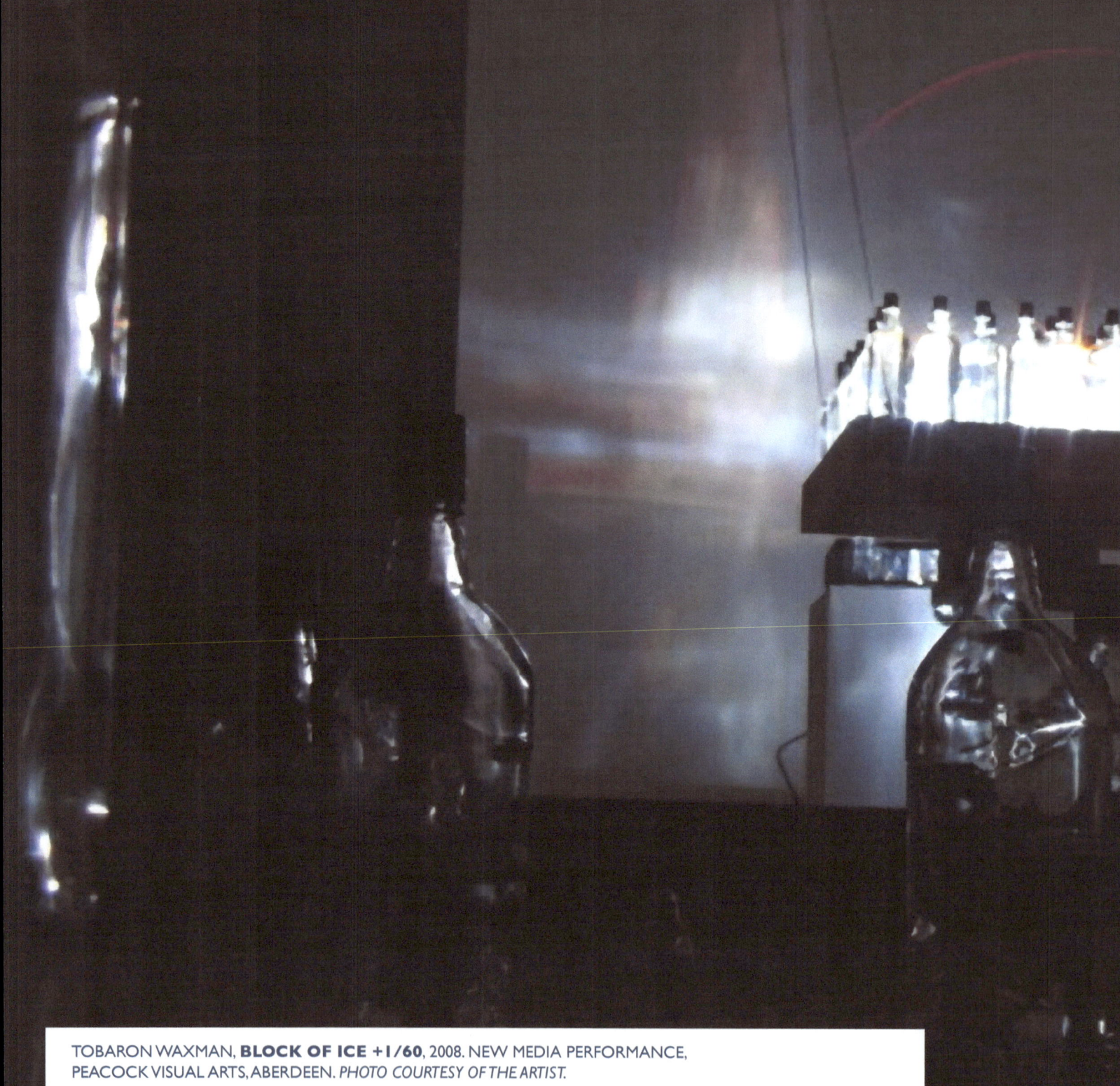

TOBARON WAXMAN, **BLOCK OF ICE +1/60**, 2008. NEW MEDIA PERFORMANCE,
PEACOCK VISUAL ARTS, ABERDEEN. *PHOTO COURTESY OF THE ARTIST.*

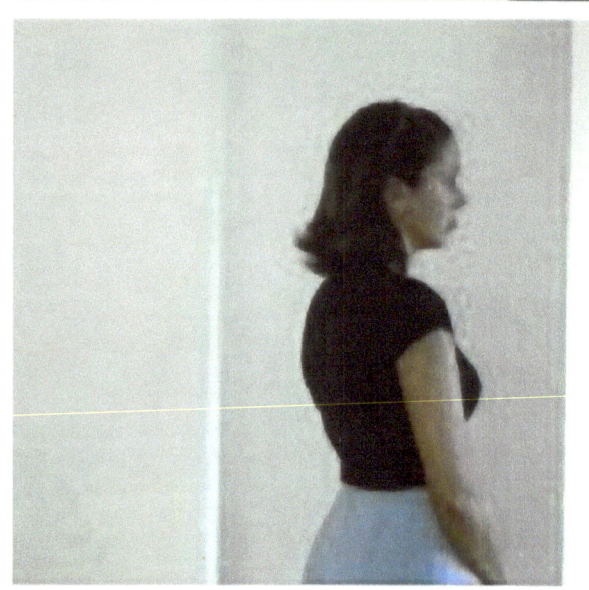
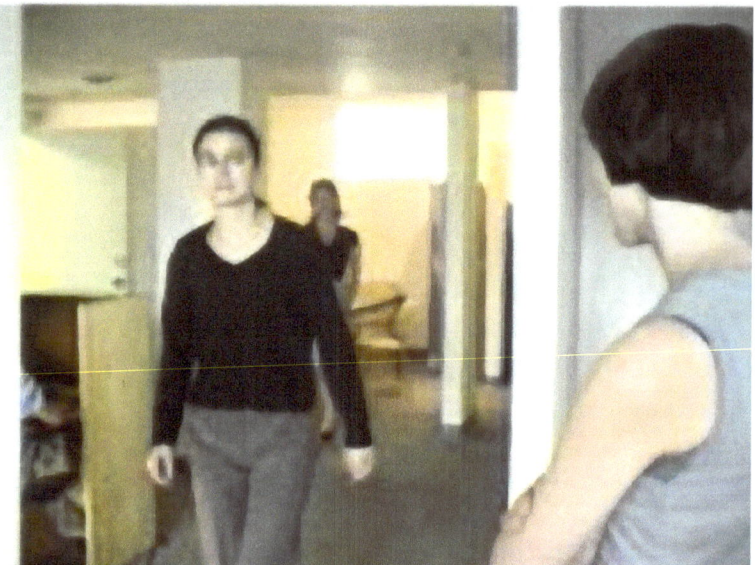
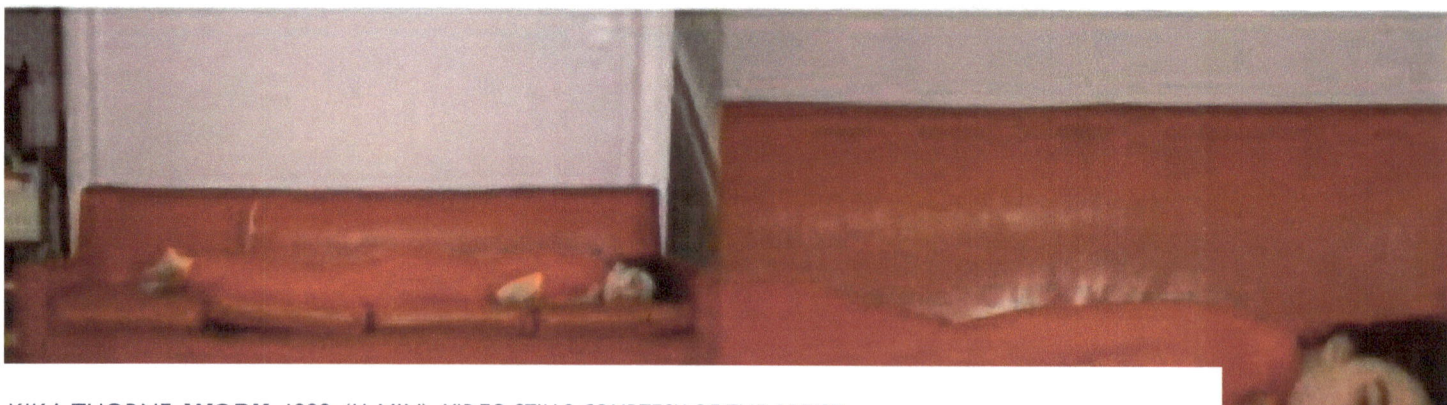

KIKA THORNE, **WORK**, 1999. (II MIN). *VIDEO STILLS COURTESY OF THE ARTIST.*

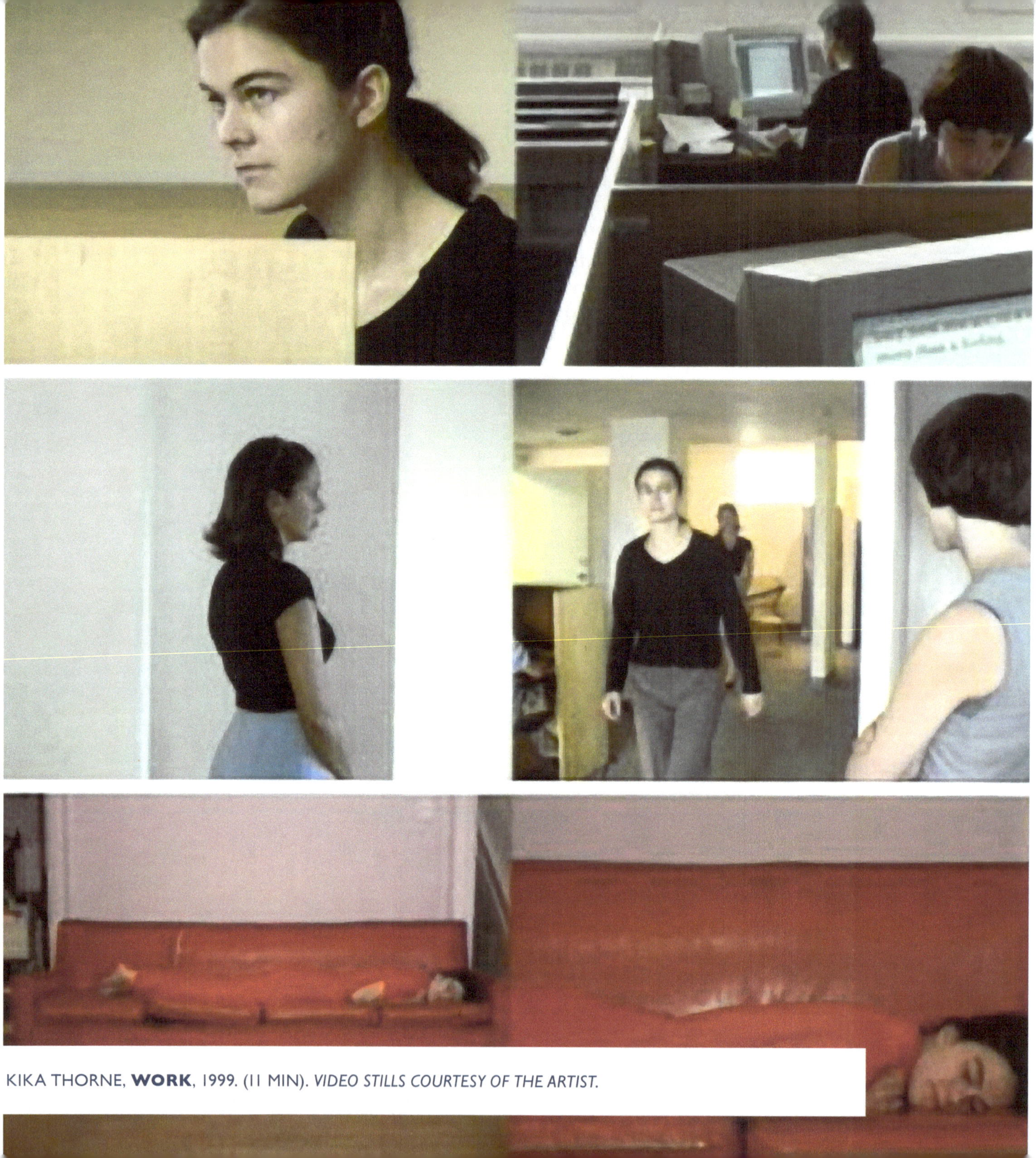

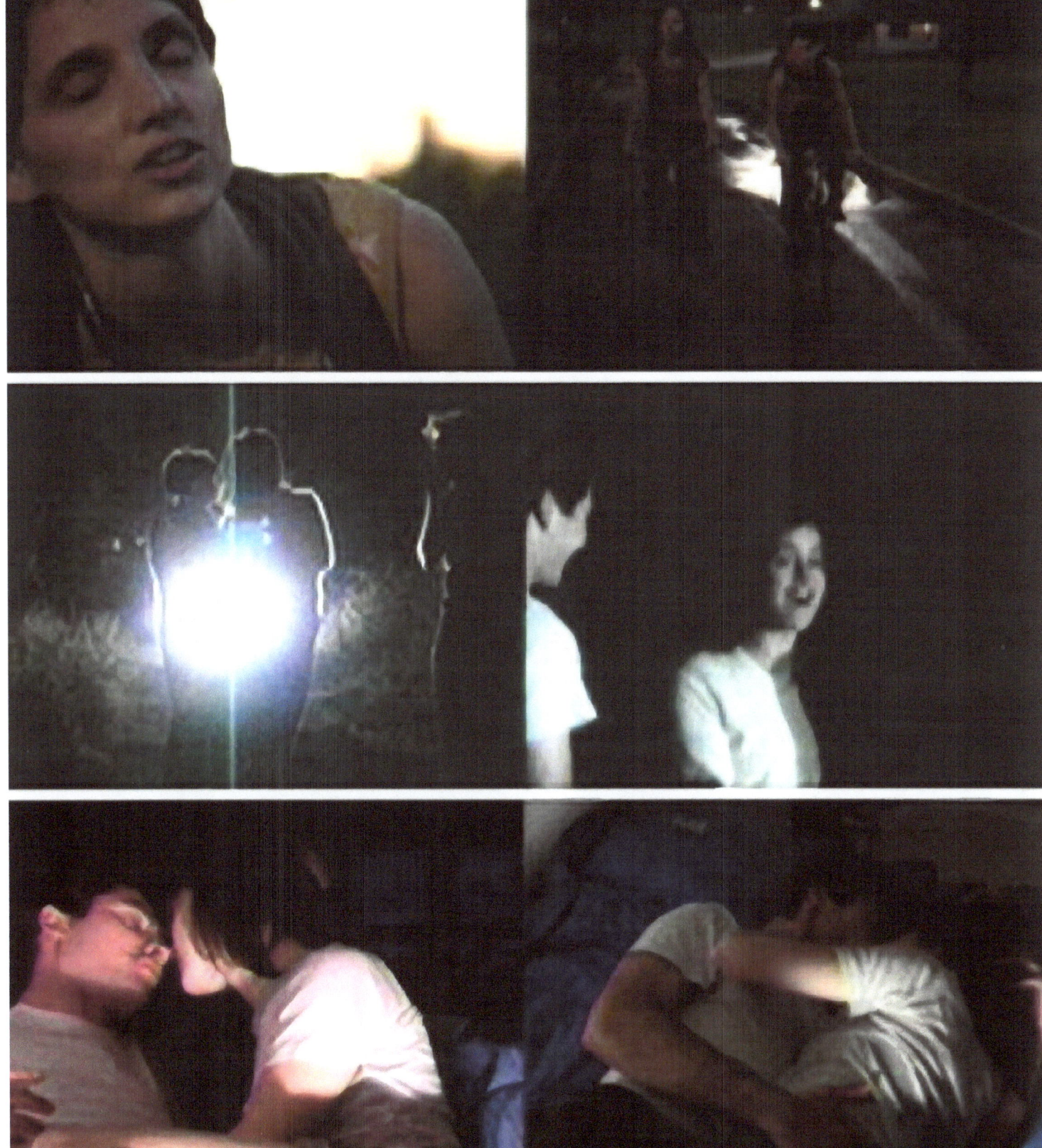

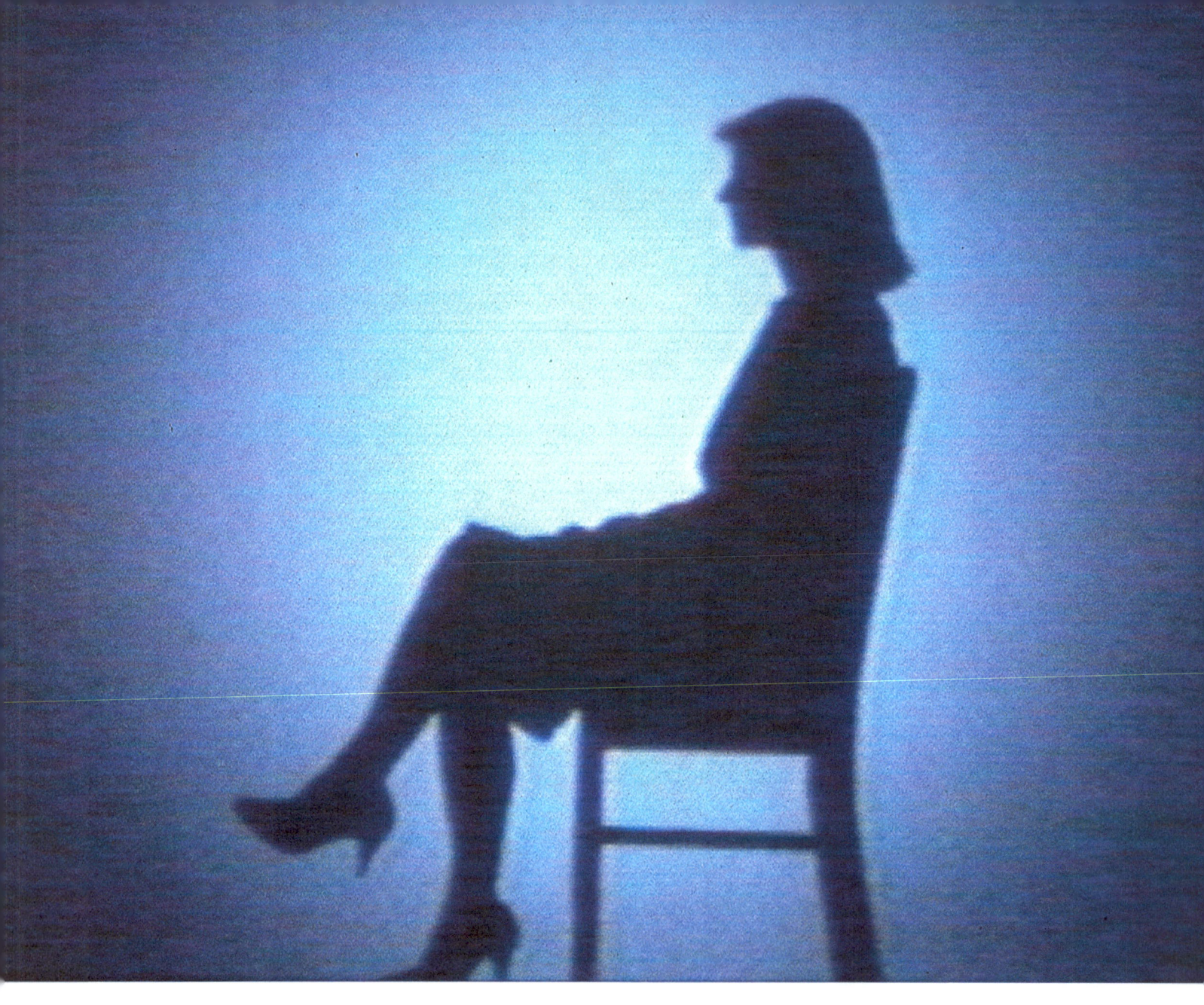

COLEEN FINLAYSON AND CHERIE MOSES, **THE MEASURE OF SUCCESS**, 1987. (3:15 MIN).
VIDEO STILL COURTESY OF THE ARTISTS.

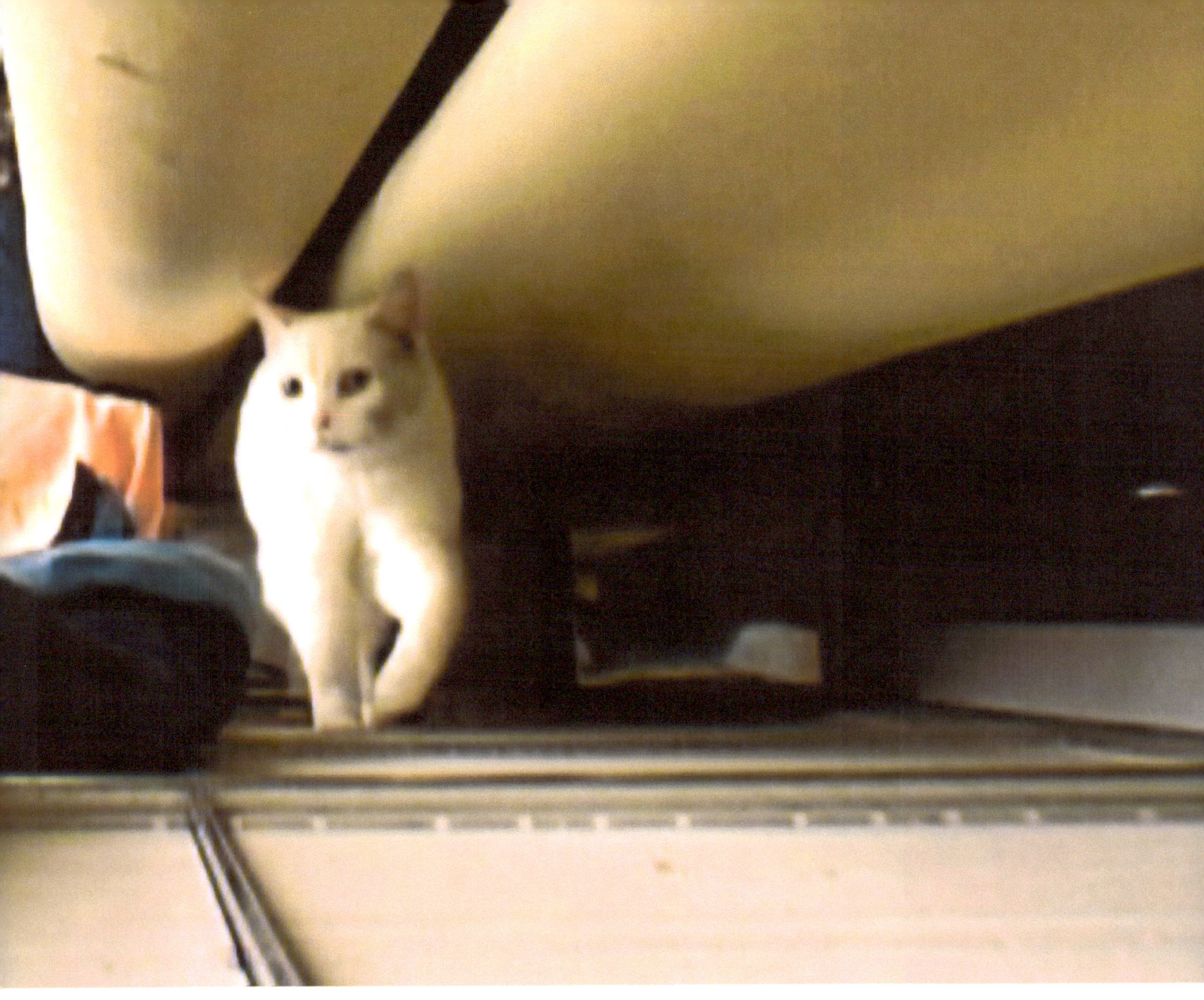

EMILY VEY DUKE & COOPER BATTERSBY, **A CURE FOR BEING ORDINARY**, 2005. (6 MIN).
VIDEO STILL COURTESY OF THE ARTISTS.

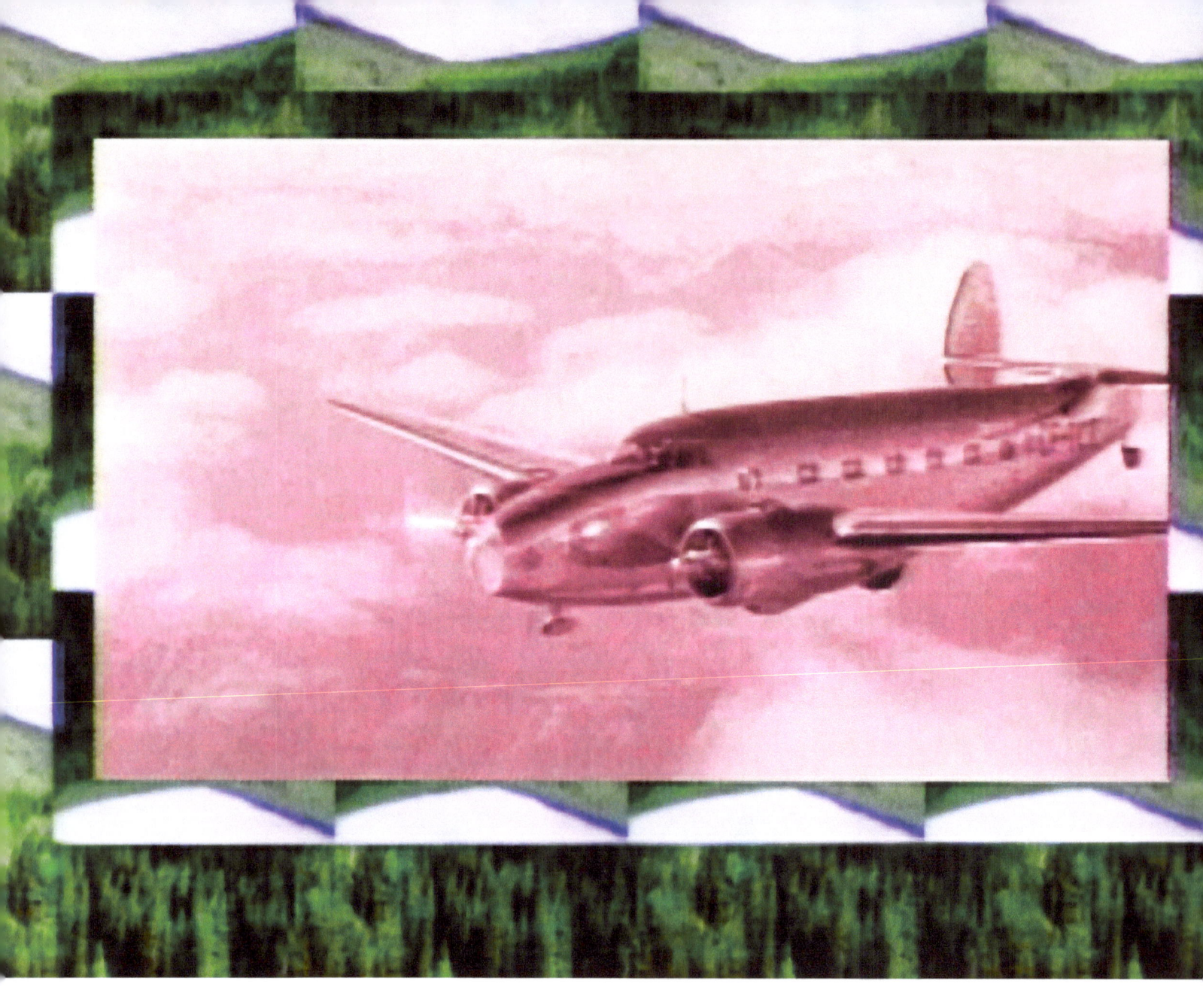

LEILA SUJIR, **THE DREAMS OF THE NIGHT CLEANERS**, 1995 (46 MIN). *VIDEO STILLS COURTESY OF THE ARTIST.*

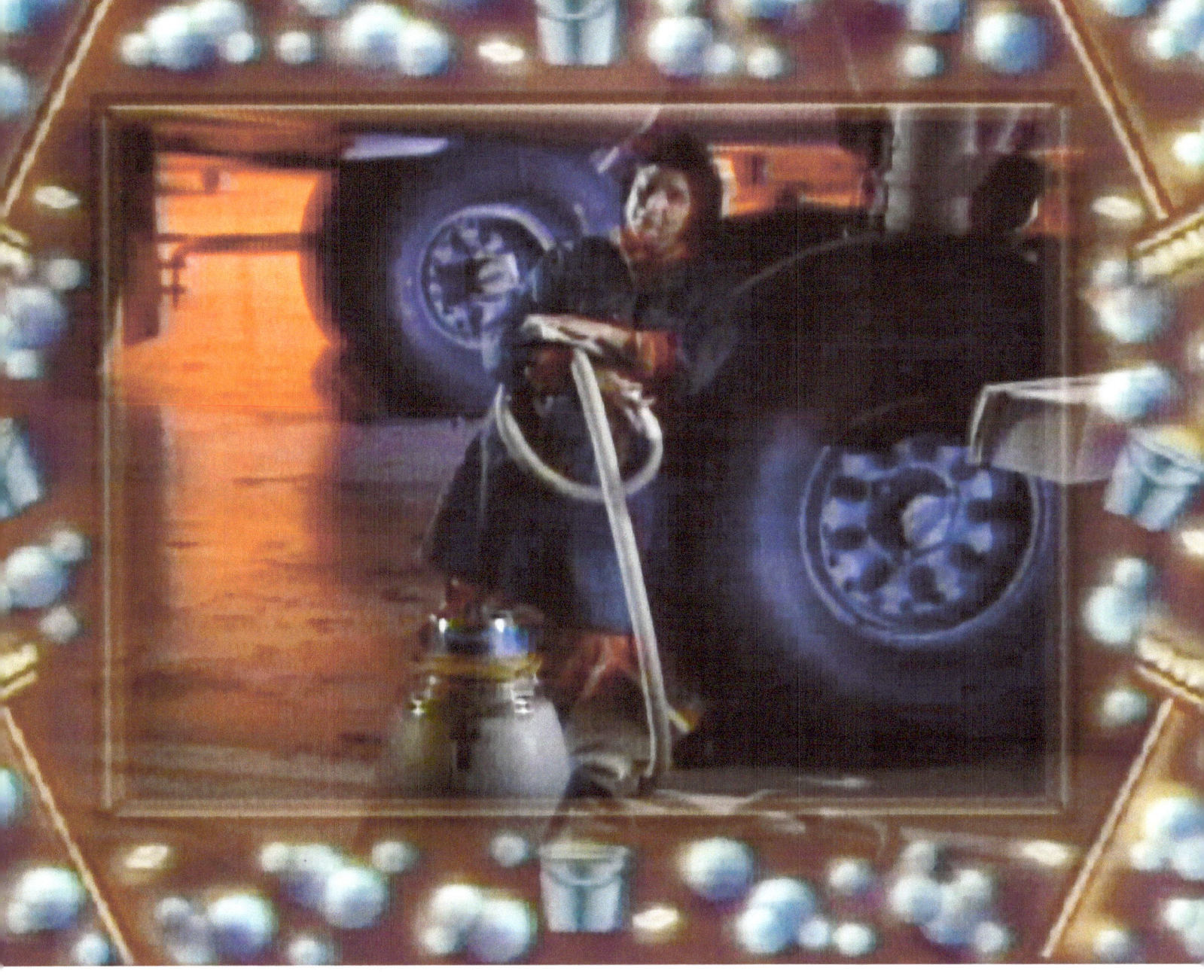

BIOGRAPHIES

AMY ALEXANDER is a software and audiovisual performance artist who has worked in film, video, and music, as well as in digital media art. Her work has been presented on the Internet, in clubs and on the street as well as in festivals and museums. She is a founder of the Runme.org software art repository, and she writes about both software in popular culture and audiovisual performance history. Her work has been performed and exhibited at venues including ISEA, Ars Electronica, Transmediale, Read Me, SIGGRAPH, and the Whitney Museum. Amy is an Associate Professor of Visual Arts at the University of California, San Diego. amy-alexander.com.

CATHY BUSBY makes art that responds to the everyday tensions of navigating contemporary life: "How am I going to get out of debt? What should I buy? What do I need? Am I having a panic attack or is this normal?" Her politically-motivated work involves making collections of things that she uses as source material in her installations and printed matter: food packaging, self-maintenance products, public apologies, university and corporate slogans, message t-shirts, neighbourhood event posters, management speak, self-help books. She has a BFA from the Nova Scotia College of Art and Design (1984) and an MA in Media Studies (1992) from Concordia University, Montreal. She was awarded a Fulbright Fellowship at New York University (1995-96). She has a PhD in Communication (1999) from Concordia University. Her recent exhibitions include in 2009: *We Are Sorry*, Melbourne and Halifax; *Your Choice*, Vancouver; in 2008: *Your Choice*, Beijing; *Righting the Wrongs*, Melbourne; *Sorry*, Sydney; *Branded*, Waterloo, Canada; in 2007: *Whatever I Like*, Beijing; *The North End*, Toronto; in 2006: *Blowback*, Public Acts, Halifax, www.publicacts.ca/act4; *The North End*, Berlin. cathybusby.ca.

JIM COLQUHOUN is an artist and writer based in Glasgow. His work seeks to negotiate the boundaries between art and life, waking and dreaming, fiction and fact. To this end he produces drawings, installations, performances and texts. He has shown recently in Edinburgh, Copenhagen, New York, Akureyri and Glasgow.

ANJA HERTENBERGER and ANJA STEIDINGER develop collaborative projects as a way of linking their friendship with artistic process and thereby transcending relationships based merely on production. Motivated by their concern for politics and quality of life, their primary topics of investigation include urban space, cooperation, and subjectivity. Hertenberger and Steidinger make use of various media and often employ the mechanics of researched-oriented experiments to formulate the content of their work. Depending on the objectives of their research projects, they may integrate any combination of performance, intervention, photography, video, and audio for data collection. Their output takes many forms, including performance lecture, interactive CD ROM, installation, video and photo documentation, text and drawing. Steidinger and Hertenberger each hold diplomas in fine arts from Hochschule für bildende Künste Hamburg. In addition, Hertenberger has completed an MFA in Interactive Media and Environments at Hanzehogeschool Groningen, the Netherlands and Steidinger is currently pursuing doctoral research into the subject of artistic research through the Faculty of Fine Arts at the University of Barcelona. anjahertenberger.net and anja-steidinger.net.

MILENA PLACENTILE is a Canadian writer and curator living in Winnipeg, Manitoba. Over the years, she has worked with various organizations including Gallery 1C03 at the University of Winnipeg, Video Pool Media Arts Centre (Winnipeg), SMART Project Space (Amsterdam), The Ottawa Art Gallery, and The Walter Phillips Gallery (Banff), among others. Holding a Master of Museum Studies from the University of Toronto, Placentile continues to investigate audience-centered curatorial practices and socially engaged cultural policy. She is a member of the International Association of Curators of Contemporary Art and she has received generous support from organizations including the Canada Council for the Arts, the Winnipeg and Manitoba Arts Councils,

the International Association of Art Critics (Armenia), and the Office of the Consul General of France (Toronto). Her recent exhibitions include *Trust Us, We're Artists* (2006), *Rehab: Weaning Youth Arts off Corporate Crack* (2007), and *The Arts of Togetherness* (2009). *Showing Up and Speaking Out* is forthcoming (2010).

Holding an MFA from Goldsmiths College, University of London, SAKI SATOM makes drawings, videos and installations that explore behavioural norms and conventional wisdom, often focusing on codes and practices that tend to go largely unnoticed. She is drawn to bland urban spaces and day-to-day social rituals. The world she presents is, on the surface, a deeply familiar one; however, in each of her works, she introduces a tone that calls all assumptions into question. Satom has recently presented solo exhibitions at Gallery Pfeister, Bornholm, Denmark (2008), Internal Audit, Camden Arts Centre, London, UK (2006), and One Severn Street, Birmingham (2005). She has also participated in numerous group shows including Asian Hot Shots Berlin, Jet and Velvet Projects, Berlin, (2009); To-Lo, Tokyo-London Art Exchange, Stephen Lawrence Gallery, London (2008); Paper Bag Lady and Other Stories, Timothy Taylor Gallery, London (2007); Drawing 2007, Drawingroom, London (2007), New Reform, Netwerk Galerij, Aalst, Belgium (2006); Tokyo-Berlin / Berlin-Tokyo, Neue Nationalgalerie, Berlin

BIOGRAPHIES CONT

(2006). Satom has participated in residencies at Camden Arts Centre, London (2006) and Tanera Mor International Artists Workshop, Scotland (2007). Born in Tokyo, Satom now lives and works in London. gasworks.org.uk/studioartists.

ABBY SCHONEBOOM is a sociologist and new media artist based at The City University of New York (CUNY). Her work focuses on "creative resistance," looking at workers who reclaim time from the labour process in order to pursue their own intellectual and artistic projects. Originally from Newcastle Upon Tyne, she studied engineering and economics at Oxford University, pursuing an IT career in the United States, where she worked as a web designer at the height of the dotcom era. Becoming interested in a critical evaluation of "boundaryless" workplaces, she achieved a PhD in sociology exploring the potential of workblogging to create social change. She is currently Assistant Professor of Sociology at the City University of New York (LaGuardia Community College), where she pursues ethnographic and multimedia-based research. In her scholarly and artistic work, Schoneboom focuses on visual sociology and new media, building on her experience as a web designer and instructional technology developer. *Project Skive* was inspired by her personal experience of America's long-hours work culture, and her concern that the UK is heading down a similar path

of self-exploitation. More of her work is featured at abbyschoneboom.com and bonkworld.org.

BRIAN SMALL is a Znet Sustainer [zmag.org/zspace/pingrin], and a lecturer at Minami Kyusyu University, Japan.

MONIKA VYKOUKAL worked until recently as curator at Peacock Visual arts, Aberdeen, Scotland, and commissioned the *No Time to Lose* exhibition and publication. Some of her formative work experiences include customer support in call centres. She is a delegate for the Industrial Workers of the World [IWW].

Based in Toronto, TOBARON WAXMAN produces work that contextualizes gender, embodiment, and the physical experience of time as systems of inscription. His work includes elements of Diaspora experience and traditional Jewish texts, music, and philosophy, as well as politics and desire. He completed an MFA at the School of the Art Institute of Chicago (2003), where he also taught Voice. Further to this, he has been a visiting artist/lecturer at UC Irvine, Parsons, SOAS, Hampshire College, and Tel Aviv University. Waxman also studies and performs Jewish liturgical music as a cantorial soloist. In 2007, he showed collaborative video/photo projects and lectured at the Berlin Volksbuhne, Videotage Hong Kong, and Tel Aviv University. He is a recipient of many awards including the Van Lier Digital Artist Residency, ACO Hong Kong Art and Culture Outreach Residency, Atlantic Center for the Arts, and Franklin Furnace Performance Art Award. His videos have screened Counting Past 2 (Toronto), Chicago Leather Archives, Mix NYC and Brasil, MoCCA Seattle, Frameline (San Francisco), Lesben Film Fest (Berlin), and VDance (Ramallah/Tel Aviv). His photographs and essays have been published in Magenta's *Carte Blanche*, *FUSE Magazine*, *Time Out Tel Aviv*, *LTTR*, *GLQ*, and others. tobaron.com.

TORU YAMAMORI is Associate Professor at Doshisha University, Kyoto, Japan, and a research associate at Capability and Sustainability Centre, Cambridge, UK.

ACKNOWLEDGMENTS

THIS EXHIBITION WAS MADE
POSSIBLE THANKS TO THE MANY
CONTRIBUTIONS OF OUR …

FUNDERS:
The Henry Moore Foundation
The Van Lier Foundation Fellowship funded by the
New York Trust, administered by Harvestworks
Hangar.org Centre de producció d'Arts Visuals
Canada Council for the Arts
The City University of New York
The Scottish Arts Council
Aberdeen City Council

PROJECT PARTNERS:
Collections Curator, Justin Parkes, and his
colleagues at The Georgina Scott Sutherland
Library, Robert Gordon University
John Edwards at Aberdeen Maritime Museum
Aberdeen Office Supplies
Philip Annand at Aberdeen City Council
William Grant & Sons

VOLUNTEERS:
Craig Barrowman
Jonathan Buckland
Jiun Jhy Her
All others who contributed so much
time and effort - thank you!

FELLOW ADVOCATES FOR
BETTER WORK/LIFE BALANCE:
Carl Honoré of slowplanet.net and carlhonore.com
John deGraaf of timeday.org

The curator, Milena Placentile, wishes to thank
Monika Vykoukal and all other members of staff at
Peacock Visual Arts for their tremendous support,
vibrant energy, warm hospitality, and collective
vision. She also expresses deepest gratitude to all
the artists and writers who shared in the realization
of this project. Finally, warm gratitude to Christen
Poulsen, cam bush, Sigrid Dahle, Anthony Kiendl,
and Glen Johnson. Thank you!

Monika Vykoukal would like to thank, in particular,
Jim Colquhoun for his serendipitous contribution, all
her colleagues, especially for their support at trying
moments, and, of course, Milena Placentile for offering
to produce this project with Peacock Visual Arts.

ONLINE
RESOURCES

PEACOCKVISUALARTS.COM
NOTIMETOLOSE. WORDPRESS.COM
DELICIOUS.COM/
NOTIMETOLOSE
FINETUNE.COM/
PLAYLIST/2242979

www.ingramcontent.com/pod-product-compliance
Lightning Source LLC
Chambersburg PA
CBHW050747180526
45159CB00003B/1376